PRESS PASS

For Jim —
A GREAT FRIEND + ONE OF THE
MOST ARTISTICALLY GIFTED !
I ALWAYS ENVIED YOU IN
HIGH SCHOOL + YOUR TALENT,
BUT REALLY APPRECIATED TAKING
ME UNDER YOUR WING.
HOPE YOU ENJOY MY BOOK.

Bobby

PRESS PASS

BY

BOB TRIMBLE

Copyright © 2016 Bob Trimble
Published by BULLITT42 Publishing

Designed by Vince Pannullo
Cover Photography by Michael D. Lackovich

Printed in the United States of America by RJ Communications.

ISBN: 978-0-578-18260-5

CONTENTS

For Kim – My wife, my best friend and partner in life. You have always been there to share in the highs and help get me through the lows. You are the inspiration to give everything I can every day.

For Ryan, Brandon and Jordan – My boys now grown into men who I have loved sharing my passion with over the years. The smiles on your faces said it all.

For my parents Bob and Mary – Thank you for giving me life, a love of sports and competition and telling me to always "follow my dreams".

FOREWARD

IT'S May of 1977 and I'm a sophomore at Ohio University in Athens. Majoring in Radio & Television Communications. I am actively involved with both ACRN (All Campus Radio Network) and WOUB-TV (The University's owned and operated television station). But there is something I yearn for that I just cannot get on campus and that is talking to athletes and coaches on their turf, not here in the Hocking Hills of southeastern Ohio.

That's when I decide to write a note indicating this desire to my hometown Pittsburgh Pirates' and their longtime Director of Public Relations, Bill Guilfoile. Mr. Guilfoile's responsibilities included a myriad of duties such as writing and editing the team's annual media guide and press notes for each home and away game. He also handled all requests from print, radio and TV outlets for credentials to report on ballgames in person.

So it is in this situation that I am pleased to find out that the Pirates will set aside a "press pass" in my name for an upcoming home contest against the Los Angeles Dodgers and their first year manager Tommy Lasorda. Press credentials are necessary to enter the stadium for access to areas off limits to fans including dressing rooms, the press box, usually located high above where the fans seating areas and luxury boxes are and of course the playing fields themselves. Since the mid 1960's as an eight or nine year old playing little league or midget football, I had dreamed of becoming a sports broadcaster and while this was only a first step it felt like a whole lot more.

Through 2005, I or the radio or television station I was working for at the time would make regular requests for game day credentials. In the years after that first Dodgers' game, I was fortunate enough to be involved covering Super Bowls, World Series, NBA and NHL Finals, Indianapolis 500's, and numerous other racing events on both the Indy and NASCAR circuits as well as a multitude of PGA, LPGA and Senior Golf Tour events. Add to that NCAA Basketball Final Fours, Bowl Games, and other collegiate and high school events and it proved to be a most exciting and fulfilling career in broadcasting.

On the upcoming pages you will hopefully get a feel for what I felt as I got to sit down with some of the biggest names in sports and entertainment in the 1970's, 80's, 90's and the early 2000's. My dad had a variety of sayings that I always kept in the back of my mind since his passing in 1971 and one of the best was, "Bobby we all put our pants on the same way, one leg at a time. Remember that. Nobody you will meet in your lifetime is any better than you are. Oh sure they may make more money or be recognized for what it is they do more than yourself, but again they are no better than you." I agree dad, but honestly, sitting across from say Muhammad Ali the very first time I met him was somewhat intimidating to say the least.

Ironically it was Ali himself who saw my tentativeness and simply said, "Go ahead Bob and ask me anything you want." I did just that and the rest as they say is history. It was a professional journey that I will treasure for as long as I live.

MUHAMMAD ALI

I guess it is fitting that of the multitude of athletes I've had the opportunity to interview over the years, I should begin alphabetically with quite probably the most visible worldwide in history, Muhammad Ali. The former heavyweight boxing champion was known by millions around the globe long before the advent of 24 hour sports networks such as ESPN. He had a charisma that wooed men and women alike and whether or not you agreed with his religious beliefs, you had to respect the courage it took to stand behind those beliefs during the tumultuous era of the 1960's.

It was there in 1967 at just twenty-five years of age that Ali (Cassius Clay at the time) was stripped of his heavyweight crown for refusing to enter the military draft and the war in Vietnam. He was already an Olympic Gold Medalist at the Rome games of 1960 and currently the heavyweight champ after disposing of the previous champion Sonny Liston. Ali said no to the draft based on those beliefs that prevented him from taking another human being's life. It is well documented what ensued, a three and a half year legal battle to regain his boxing license and quite literally his life.

Muhammad went on to regain his title not once, but twice before retiring permanently in 1981. And it was just two years after that when I first encountered the man simply known as "The Greatest".

It was the spring of 1983 in Kalamazoo, Michigan and I was working as a radio salesperson for WKFR-FM and WKNR-AM in Battle Creek. Yes it's the same Battle Creek that is home to Kelloggs cereals. Ali, who at the time was living not too far away along Lake Michigan in the town of Berrien Springs was in town for a visit with his friend and longtime boxing official Henry Grooms. Mr. Grooms had invited him to take a look at some of the young up and coming Golden Gloves talent in the area. He was accompanied by CBS television journalist Bill Kurtis and his TV crew as part of a documentary on the former champ's life.

I was on hand having been invited by one of the real greats of broadcasting in the state of Michigan, Bob Sherman. Bob, who has since passed away, was for years the radio voice of the Indianapolis 500. But he was also a huge fight fan and when this opportunity presented itself he jumped at the chance to sit down with Ali.

Once Bob and Muhammad had completed about a twenty minute interview, the ever gracious Mr. Sherman took time to introduce me to Ali and with my own microphone and tape recorder I too was able to ask questions of him. A point to remember here is that I still was not employed as an accredited member of the media. I was just a young man who was in the right place at the right time to talk with the most visible athlete of my generation and he was cordial enough to take the time to chat.

BOB & MUHAMMAD ALI

To this day I remember that interview like it was yesterday. We all talked after Muhammad had actually gotten in the ring for a little light sparring with the young Golden Gloves members. Slowed by age and what were the beginning signs of his Parkinson's Syndrome, he nonetheless put on a display for the few of us in attendance that was pretty special. Those quick feet still seemed quick as ever and his right then left then right then left were showstoppers for all of us. Sadly when he came out of the ring showered in sweat, while he toweled off it was easy to see how the years in the ring had taken their toll on his now near forty year old body.

"If you had taken more than 50,000 shots to the head over the years you'd be a little punchy too." said Ali to me with a smile. Humor was one of Muhammad's trademarks every bit as much as his talents with the gloves. He went on to answer every one of my questions with a sincerity and warmth I've only experienced with two other athletes, "Mr. Hockey", Gordie Howe and former Detroit Tiger Alan Trammell who I will profile later.

Ali, like many elite athletes could tell you about each and every fight he had and what were the keys or the turning points. From his much bally-hooed and promoted encounters with Joe Frazier, George Foreman, Ken Norton and Larry Holmes, I learned what Muhammad was thinking and attempting to do in those bouts. He readily admitted that his famed "rope-a-dope" tactic to have the clearly superior at the time Foreman punch himself out worked to perfection. However, the toll it took on Ali's body was far more than he had ever imagined.

Eleven years later and now in Detroit as the Weekend Sports Anchor and Weekday Sports Reporter for WKBD UPN-50 television, I again would have the chance of speaking with Muhammad Ali. This time my three young sons would have the opportunity as well.

One of the early WCW shows was coming to the Motor City's Joe Louis Arena, and on this day a press conference was being held to promote the event. I was assigned to cover the presser and once I realized who would be on hand for the only time in my professional life, I asked if my family could attend as well.

At the time my oldest sons Ryan and Brandon were ten and nine years old respectively and our new baby Jordan was just 4 months of age. I asked and was given the ok by the event organizers to bring the kids down to meet Muhammad in the "green room" backstage along with a pair of individuals the boys knew well from the "Rocky" movies, Hulk Hogan and Mr. T. Immediately upon entering what is the arena's "Olympia Club", the older boys were in total awe. Hogan and Mr. T. warmly greeted them and made them comfortable. A few minutes later, Ali began performing some of his famous slight of hand magic and this went on for about 10 minutes.

Then Ali turned towards me and I said, "I'm sure you don't remember me champ, but I sure remember you and how nice you were to me." Ali replied now in a very soft whisper, "Kalamazoo." The Parkinson's had since robbed this once great communicator of his speech, but not his mind. I am convinced Muhammad was "all there" if you will inside his damaged body. He simply could not communicate his thoughts as well due to the disease. But how great was it that he remembered me? It was just amazing.

ALI HOLDING BABY JORDAN

ALI, BRANDON, JORDAN & RYAN

He then pointed towards little Jordan lying in his portable carrier atop the bar and motioned as if trying to say, "May I hold him?" I readily agreed and to this day the photo of Muhammad Ali holding my child and planting a kiss on his cheek is one of our family's most celebrated possessions.

And I celebrate having spent a few treasured moments with "The Greatest" who famously said, "Don't count the days, make the days count!" I for one believe he certainly did. His passing at the age of 74 in June of 2016 was felt around the globe & without question to me personally.

GEORGE
"SPARKY"ANDERSON

ONE of my longtime acquaintances in professional sports was the former manager of the Cincinnati Reds and later the Detroit Tigers, George "Sparky" Anderson. I first met him in the summer of 1977 in his office inside the visiting dressing room at Pittsburgh's Three Rivers Stadium when he was skippering the Reds for a series against my hometown Pirates.

A few months earlier I was in this same dressing room for the very first time in my career getting to speak with rookie manager Tommy Lasorda and members of his Los Angeles Dodgers. It was my initial encounter ever with microphone in hand as a member of the ACRN (All Campus Radio Network), so this meeting was a lot less stressful for me. I came in knowing what to expect and exactly what I wanted to talk to Sparky about.

We spent a good twenty minutes together before he was summoned into another part of the dressing room by one of his coaches and as he left he said, "Bobby make sure and drop by after the game if you have any other questions and I hope you enjoy it. And tell all the good folks in Athens at Ohio U. I said hello if I don't see you." That was Sparky.

He was very easy going and always had time or made time to speak with members of the media, especially those who eventually covered his team on a regular basis. From his white hair to all of his little idiosyncrasies, such as refusing to step on the foul line when entering or leaving the field on the countless occasions he set out to replace his pitcher, Sparky was most of all fun to be around and his passing in 2010 was a very sad day for me, much like that of Ali.

I in fact did eventually become a regular in the Detroit Tigers dressing room and at Tiger Stadium where Sparky moved in 1979. From my days in Lansing, Toledo, Grand Rapids and finally Detroit itself, Sparky and I crossed paths hundreds of times at games, charity functions and awards dinners and that big smile directed towards me was always welcomed.

While working as Sports Director for WZZM-TV, the ABC affiliate in Grand Rapids, the marketing director for the station came up with a promotional idea involving me called "One on One with Bob Trimble". The platform has been used in many markets before and since with the TV personality (me), challenged at a particular sport by viewers each week.

And sometimes professionals got the itch to challenge ol' Bobby T. like the granddaughter and grandson of the late leader of the Flying Wallenda's, Karl. There I went up and up, some 25 feet above the ground to attempt to walk the high wire. Attempt was a good word and we'll leave it at that. I also mud wrestled a 275 pound woman, had a softball home run hitting contest with the Grand Rapids' Chief of Police, raced go-karts with Indy Car pros such as Bobby Rahal, Paul Tracy and Scott Brayton and even had the honor of getting my butt kicked in squash by United States Senator Carl Levin.

Now I never got to do anything specific with the Tigers, yet on the team's annual caravan around the state of Michigan at the beginning of the 1988 season, who should I see coming out of the hotel carrying his very own "One on One with Bob Trimble" t-shirt but Sparky! We had some laughs that day and many others and I remained a huge admirer of the "Main Spark". Not because of his accomplishments as a major league manager, having won World Series in both the American and National League with Detroit and Cincinnati, but rather because of his engaging personality. He was a man who absolutely enjoyed his profession and was happy to spread that enjoyment to all that would listen.

BOB & SPARKY ANDERSON
AT SPRING TRAINING IN LAKELAND, FL

I am so happy and proud I was able to listen and take away many positive memories from my friend Sparky. The last of which came on the day
in 2000 when it was announced he had been selected for his rightful place
in Cooperstown & the Baseball Hall of Fame. I was working at EMPIRE
at the time and realized that the three hour time difference between Buffalo
and Thousand Oaks, California where Sparky resided could make for some
perfect timing for an interview on this special day. If I could reach him
through what was certain to be a back-up of calls and well wishes, would
he agree to come on "live" during the evening's FAN-TV program that I
was hosting?

Well there was only one way to find out so from my home before
heading into work, I called him and to my amazement got through fairly
quickly as his wife answered. I mentioned who I was and asked if Sparky
had a quick moment for me to congratulate him. Mrs. Anderson turned

from the phoned and shouted, "George, Bob Trimble is on the line to say hi." Within seconds his familiar voice popped on and said, "Bobby how are ya kid?" I responded with something to the effect of, "I'm just fine, but I would hazard a guess you are feeling quite a bit better." He started to laugh and agreed he was thrilled to be selected for the Hall. I then requested him to come on for five to 10 minutes later in the day for my show and he did not hesitate to say yes.

What transpired that night was our final interview and with my questions & those of some of our viewers, Sparky's responses could not have been more interesting or heartfelt. What made it even more special for me was the fact I was able to have one of the most important men in my life back home in Pittsburgh get through on the line to ask Sparky a question.

John Bickerton was and remains my favorite teacher ever and it goes without saying a longtime close friend. He is an encyclopedia of America's Pastime and I have sat next to him at many a Pirates' game over the years watching him scribble in his scorebook each inning. Talk about passion, this has been going on since the 1950's.

So on this one very special night, it proved a perfect cross country convergence getting together with Sparky & Bic. I cannot remember another time in all my years in front of the camera that was more proud and pleased. Thanks guys.

JEROME "THE BUS" BETTIS

AUGUST 8, 2015 marked a culmination of sorts for me with the long awaited enshrinement of running back Jerome Bettis into the Pro Football Hall of Fame.

I was among the thousands on hand at Tom Benson Stadium along with my son Jordan to watch as "The Bus" took his place among the greatest players in league history. It is a ceremony that has grown unbelievably since the days when the inductions and speeches took place in front of a much smaller, but no less enthusiastic crowd on the steps in front of the Hall itself. It has become quite a production and as always many previous Hall of Famers come back to Canton to rekindle friendships and of course take part up on the massive stage.

The first induction ceremony I ever attended as a cub reporter for Ohio University was 1977 when I watched as Frank Gifford, Forrest Gregg, Gale Sayers, Bart Starr and Bill Willis officially entered the Hall. It was incredible sitting in the very first row and getting interviews with all of them to take back to Athens.

JEROME BETTIS

Now back in Canton with my son who was actually older than I was at that time, it felt like coming full circle after some thirty eight years. Wow! But the common thread was out mutual love of football and admiration for Bettis.

I was born in the Pittsburgh area (Jerome's primary career was of course with the Steelers after a couple of seasons with the Rams). He was born in Detroit (where I worked for some seven years at WKBD-TV in suburban Southfield where Jerome's brother John was heading up Jerome

Bettis Enterprises). And finally we first met at Notre Dame while he was a freshman thanks to a coaching friend of mine who as Howard Cosell used to say, "Matriculated to South Bend" that very same season. It really is a small world when you think about it in those terms.

What you see with Bettis is really what you get. He is a terrific competitor who genuinely enjoys himself in almost any situation. Whether it's showing off his exceptional skills in bowling, or his days of "bowling" over the likes of Bears' Linebacker Brian Urlacher on a snowy afternoon at Heinz Field, his smile is just contagious. I clearly remember after bursting through a hole for a tough first down or following one of his 94 career rushing touchdowns, "The Bus" jumping up and forward shaking his head smiling as if to say, "Better get used to this because I am just going to keep coming at you".

Jerome is a classic example of a young man driven to succeed thanks to his own talents and the love and support of his family where both mother AND father were there for guidance and support. His was a special family that is honestly unusual in this day and age for inner city children. Unfortunately it is a sign of the times that the mother is all too often left to raise and support her children as the father of those same children shuns his responsibilities and for all intents and purposes simply disappears. Such was not the case for Jerome Bettis.

From Detroit's Mackenzie High School to Notre Dame and eventually the Steelers, he drove himself both physically and mentally to conquer the obstacles in his path towards success both as a ballplayer and individual. He is always quick to point out those that assisted in even the smallest way on his climb to the top of the National Football League. Respect is what he gives and it is returned in many ways on a regular basis.

No time was this more evident than when the Steelers arrived in Detroit for Super Bowl XXXX. As a tribute to their leader, the entire roster strode off the plane wearing green number 6 jerseys in honor of Jerome's playing days for the Fighting Irish. He led the team off the flight in the hanger and was caught completely by surprise when his teammates, led by linebacker Joey Porter, walked down the stairs looking like fifty-two Bettis's in unison.

JEROME BETTIS, BOB & JORDAN

Several years prior to finally getting to and winning a Super Bowl (in his hometown no less), I had him on our set in suburban Detroit for an interview as I had learned he was in town for a brief family visit. Ironically I had just returned from doing a story on the Rodeo being in town and had Jordan in tow to hang out behind the scenes. That's when he first met "The Bus" and when I mentioned to Jerome I was planning on bringing he and his brothers and several cousins to the upcoming Steelers' Training Camp, he put me in touch with a team assistant of his to set up passes for the day. After practice at the beautiful setting that is St. Vincent College in Latrobe, he would then bring us "inside" the roped off public area and take some time for photos and autographs with my gang. Very nice gesture and something all the kids will never forget.

There was much discussion regarding Jerome's credentials for worthiness to make the grade into the Hall of Fame. The biggest obstacle was his yards per carry average which is the lowest of any running back to make it to Canton. But what Hall voters needed to understand was that it was

NOT the yards per carry average to focus on, but rather the upswing in confidence thanks to his leadership that transformed the Steelers back to the glory of their winning ways of the 1970's. It was something that was sadly missing throughout the 80's and early 90's until his arrival in a trade from the Rams.

As popular as ever with his smile and easy going manner, Jerome Bettis remains a Pittsburgh and football icon as well as a model for young athletes everywhere.

BJORN BORG &
JIMMY CONNORS

MEN'S professional tennis in the 1970's had some of the biggest names the sport has ever produced. The United States had the likes of Arthur Ashe, the only African American to capture the men's final at Wimbledon when he did so in 1975. Also the irrepressible John McEnroe, gentlemanly Stan Smith and the always fun loving but very demanding Jimmy Connors.

Internationally the 1970's poster boy was Sweden's Bjorn Borg. With his long blond hair flying in the wind he was the game's first rock star. Borg delivered five consecutive Wimbledon titles from 1976 thru 1980 along with six French Opens proving to be adept on any surface.

Connors meantime had his own rock star appeal as he captured a total of eight Grand Slam titles including five U.S. Opens, two Wimbledon titles and one Australian Open. His career lasted much longer than Borg's and one of his brightest moments came in 1991 at the age of 39 when he reached the semi-finals of the U.S. Open.

In Jimmy's prime years from 1974 thru 1978, he and Borg met a dozen times with Connors prevailing in eight of those meetings.

BOB & BJORN BORG

Following retirement Connors helped found a highly successful Over 30 Tour that saw the likes of he, Borg, McEnroe and others crisscross the country to entertain a whole new generation of tennis fans. This is where I met the two of them as they battled all week in suburban Detroit to face each other in yet another singles final. This time on a much smaller scale, however, of approximately 2500 fans in a temporary venue.

Well into their 40's at the time, both men were still very much athletic enough to make some amazing shots in a slower paced more serve and volley game than they used to play in their heydays. Jimmy would be victorious in three sets and afterwards both men were exceptionally comfortable to talk to.

Borg was much more open about his life and career than he was when I first interviewed him at an athletic store promotional appearance in Grand Rapids in 1985. He was candid about some of his personal issues away from the court and very open about his thoughts on his opponents over the years. Clearly Jimmy Connors was his primary nemesis and while you don't always find respect and admiration for your opposition, in the case of Borg, he felt all that and more for Connors.

Likewise Conners had passionate feelings regarding his on-court encounters with Borg and stated so to me. Without question while both men entered play focused on winning their matches all over the world, no matter what the end result was, they had fun taking part in the competition. But the obvious difference between the two men was Connors' open intensity. Like McEnroe he wore his emotions on his sleeve and on more than one occasion found himself in trouble with officials. Borg approached matches with no less concentration and will to win, he just managed to do so in a calmer and more gentlemanly manner.

BOB & JIMMY CONNORS

Once we were finished talking and the camera lights were turned off, I had the pleasure of introducing my wife Kim to both men and as she snapped a few candid photos. For obvious reasons Kim could not always be on hand for my work, but when she could it was a great feeling to have her by my side and get to see the side of athletes and coaches that frankly most people don't.

From Jimmy Connors and his two fisted backhand and grunts on each and every serve or ground stroke to Bjorn Borg's quiet assassin type approach to the game, these two tennis greats proved at least on this occasion that the competition dialed down a notch still could provide thrills for all of us in attendance.

SCOTTY BOWMAN

THE head coach with the most victories in National Hockey League history is Hall of Famer Scotty Bowman. His numbers are quite staggering with 1244 regular season wins and 223 more in the Stanley Cup Playoffs. Add to that his 12 Stanley Cup Championships (9 as a head coach and 3 as a member of the front office) and you can see this man knows his hockey.

He also knows how to keep the media at arms' length and did so over the course of his storied career with St. Louis, Montreal, Buffalo, Pittsburgh, Detroit and finally Chicago.

I met Scotty for the first time while he was in the middle of his highly successful run with the Red Wings in the 1990's in Detroit. I then got to know him better when I was a member of the EMPIRE Sports Network team based in suburban Buffalo, New York. Bowman it turns out lived less than five miles away from my home in a simple, but stately residence along the Transit Valley Country Club Golf Course in East Amherst.

He was utilized by the network for his commentary on the Stanley Cup Playoffs involving the hometown Buffalo Sabres when Detroit was no longer a part of the playoff race. Overall he is a very quiet individual and very thoughtful when he does offer his expertise on the game. He is not however, someone you immediately feel comfortable speaking with as I believe he's testing you to see if you know what you're talking about or just trying to get him to say something meaningful.

For whatever reason he and I seemed to click from the start and I always got a wink or a nod when I'd see him at different venues from games to practices to the studio and especially for what we call "live shots". Live shots are when you as a reporter are at a designated location to report "live" on a game either pre or post event or really anywhere your producer wants to go "live" from.

The best example of the relationship I had with Scotty came early in the 2001-02 season when former Sabres' Hall of Fame goaltender Dominik Hasek was beginning his first season with the Red Wings following his trade. Buffalo wanted to dump Hasek's fat contract and going to a very strong Detroit team almost assured him of his goal of at last winning a Stanley Cup. For the record "The Dominator" had his best season ever with 41 wins against only 15 defeats and Detroit indeed captured the coveted Cup icing the Carolina Hurricanes.

Knowing how high profile Hasek was in Buffalo and all the hoopla surrounding his trade, I approached our executive producer John Demerle with the idea of heading over to Detroit to do a feature package on Dominik in his new home. The premise would be to feature interviews from he and his new teammates leading up to the game that night, his first against his old mates. We would be "live" pre-game with Sabres' General Manager Darcy Regier then "live" post- game with a taped interview with Scotty as well as a complete game recap.

BOB & SCOTTY BOWMAN

The Wings won the game with Hasek in net and afterwards it was time to get reaction from the respective dressing rooms. Bowman, who was an absolute control freak on every aspect of his team, had a clock installed in the Detroit dressing room that literally counted down the time you as a reporter had to get your interviews after the game then would be escorted out by members of the club's media relations department. There were no exceptions. And Scotty knew how to use that clock to his advantage, making sure he came out to speak to the media with only a few minutes to go.

When he did come out the horde of some 25 radio, TV, print journalists and camerapersons descended upon him. But he had news for everyone except me and my cameraperson. I had arranged earlier to speak with him so while I got his exclusive first post-game comments on the play of his team, his new goaltender and his old team from Buffalo, the others waited. The timing was perfect as we got our answers and quickly inserted them into my game recap package. We were the only Buffalo station in attendance and so it felt good to help EMPIRE live up to its motto of the best and most complete sports coverage in Western New York!

I felt somewhat vindicated that even the hometown Detroit media got dissed in favor of me. You see I left the Motor City on not the best of terms with my old station WKBD-TV. The new News Director Tom Bell and I had the exact opposite relationship of that of Scotty and myself. We never quite saw eye to eye on my role taking over for the legendary Ray Lane who had recently retired. I soon followed, not retired, but fired by Bell, who was a mousey little guy who was very secretive with his actions and motives keeping all in his newsroom on edge. We disagreed on numerous occasions about how stories or situations should be handled and the most blatant involved these same Red Wings in the midst of celebrating their 1996 - 97 Stanley Cup.

On this evening six days after winning the Cup, the team had assembled then dispersed from playing a full day of golf before players went their separate ways for the off-season. Several players hired limousines to take them to and from the course and one such group involved veteran

Russian players Vladimir Konstantinov and Slava Fetisov as well as their good friend, the team's massage therapist and fellow Russian, Sergei Mnatsakanov.

Little did the threesome know that the man driving them away from the course, Richard Gnida, was drunk and the ensuing crash of the limo left Konstantinov & Mnatsakanov permanently disabled while Fetisov was very lucky to be able to make a full recovery from his injuries.

I was anchoring the sports that Friday night and once word starting leaking into the newsroom both the sports and news staff began the process of getting information confirmed to be broadcast. We would cut in "live" to regular programming with the facts once we had them, but the trouble was we were getting conflicting reports from the scene. Bell, meanwhile wanted to cut in before we had confirmation and I argued to the point I know this cost me my job. Reluctantly I went on stating Fetisov and Konstantinov were both seriously injured in the crash, but that Mnatsakanov had died from his injuries. I knew in my heart I was wrong and to this day despise Bell for making me go on the air against my own better judgement.

Fortunately Sergei survived his horrific brain injury, though in a severely incapacitated state. I on the other hand never looked at Bell or WKBD-TV the same and was gone from the station some seven months later headed to Buffalo.

I never brought this story up to Scotty, though I sometimes wondered if he didn't already know. You see that is one of his gifts, Scotty Bowman pretty much knows everything there is to know about hockey and specifi-cally anything involving his own teams.

I came to know him and respect him even though he was certainly not the most approachable of personalities. I believe he respected me as a broadcaster and journalist. I remain very proud of that and feel strongly that respect helped me in many situations in my career to get the job done and done correctly.

TERRY BRADSHAW & WILLIE STARGELL

FORMER Pittsburgh Steelers Quarterback Terry Bradshaw and Pittsburgh Pirates First Baseman Willie Stargell are to the Steel City what the Statue of Liberty is to New York and the Golden Gate Bridge is to San Francisco.

They are icons that represented Pittsburgh for a total of 35 years between them. In 1979, the Steelers were Super Bowl champions of the National Football League and the Pirates captured the World Series in Major League Baseball. Because of this, they remain to this day, the central figures as part of the "City of Champions".

I interviewed both men multiple times in the 1970's, 80's and 90's and have strong, positive memories of those meetings everywhere from Three Rivers Stadium to Taylor, Michigan's Gibralter Cards Shows. As a native of suburban Pittsburgh I can say without hesitation these are two of my all-time favorites to talk to, but for different reasons.

Let's begin with Bradshaw, the blond bomber from Louisiana Tech who once was said not to have known how to spell the word cat if you spotted him the "c" and the "a". That statement came from the mouth of former Dallas Cowboys' linebacker Thomas "Hollywood" Henderson the week prior to Super Bowl XIII.

Yet it was Henderson who went on to sell his Super Bowl XII ring due to drug and money issues, so I wouldn't take what he had or has to say too much to heart. I will however, give credit where credit is due as Henderson has turned his life around and is a minister in Texas these days having won the state lottery not once, but twice.

Back to Terry who is every bit the happy go lucky, smiling , cheery guy you see on your television screens each Sunday morning during the football season. The FOX NFL Sunday panel with Curt Menefe, Howie Long,

Michael Strahan, Terry and coach Jimmy Johnson are must see television, at least for yours truly. That group's unscripted banter and unquestioned game insights make it fun and informative at the same time.

And don't let his southern drawl fool you, he is a very intelligent and articulate man. In recent years Bradshaw has spoken for the first time about living with depression, something I myself dealt with following a heart attack in 2012.

Depression doesn't distinguish between a millionaire former pro athlete and television personality or the average Joe hunkered down in his lazy boy chair with a beer and sandwich watching football in his den. It can knock you to your knees and only a personal commitment to learn to deal with it can get you back on your feet. I will say this, Terry masked his inner demons quite well. I honestly in my meetings with him formally and informally, never sensed anything but a real, honest and fun loving guy to be around. He never showed the hurt that he was experiencing behind the scenes.

TERRY BRADSHAW, BOB & GREG GUMBEL

He always called me "Hoss" when we met and asked how I'd been and where I was working at that particular time. He really has a great memory and even greater personality. When talking with him early in his career with the Steelers he was very open with the media, almost to the point of setting himself up for a fall if he failed.

Well he did that more times than not up to and including the 1974 campaign when he lost his starting job to begin the season, only to regain it and go on to lead Pittsburgh to the first of the team's four Super Bowl victories during his 14 year tenure.

He rightfully held a grudge against fans in those early years as they even cheered when he suffered injuries including a very painful separated shoulder at Three Rivers Stadium. He spoke of those times and how it made him a stronger person, one able to then enjoy even more the fruits of his amazing success and that of the team's.

Four Super Bowl wins in six years and now two more since his retirement give the Steelers the top spot in history for those NFL championships. And Terry Bradshaw was there from the very start of that success.

Pittsburgh's other legend is Willie Stargell who's career paralleled Bradshaw's time wise. He got to Pittsburgh actually eight years earlier in 1962, and retired one year before Terry in 1982. In between, "Pops", as he was known in his later years was the heart and soul of the Pirates' franchise.

Few professional teams ever had a leader both on and off the field like Stargell. His numbers earned him induction into Baseball's Hall of Fame in 1988 and he'll best be remembered for taking the Sister Sledge song, "We are Family" in 1979 and adopting it as the team's rallying cry on the way to the World Series crown that year over Baltimore.

His career was marked primarily not only for his home runs, but rather the mammoth manner in which those homers hit the stands or in several cases like Dodger Stadium, actually left the stadium! He finished up with 475 round trippers, but had he not played a great deal of his career at old Forbes Field he may have well challenged Babe Ruth's then record of 714.

BOB & WILLIE STARGELL

Forbes was cavernous to say the least, a pitcher's paradise and a home run hitter's nightmare. It was at least to dead centerfield where the distance from home plate was some 457 feet. Compare that to today's miniature parks like the Pirates' new home of PNC Park and the difference is noticeable, 47 feet to be exact. So many of Willie's long fly ball outs to the warning track would have been "long gone" into the seats today.

"Pops" had a deep baritone voice and he spoke ever so slowly to make his points clear and concise. In all the years I never saw Willie get mad at himself or a teammate or the opposition. He had tremendous composure and was a teacher in the truest sense of the word. The "Stargell Stars" he handed out to teammates for something positive they did only helped to endear him more to the team and the fans.

He passed away from complications following a stroke on April 9, 2001. Ironically that was Opening Day for the Pirates at PNC Park and the day a statute was unveiled of Stargell outside the park's leftfield entrance. I feel fortunate that of all the places the Pirates' organization could have placed my family name's brick as part of a plan to surround PNC Park, it ended up in the shadow of Willie's bronze statue.

Terry Bradshaw and Willie Stargell were two of the finest to ever play their respective sports. And for me personally, having been privileged enough to be able to sit down with both men, they indeed were the perfect duo to represent the city of Pittsburgh and its sporting tradition.

LOMAS BROWN &
CHRIS SPIELMAN

T HE primary city that my sports broadcasting career centered around was Detroit. With stops in Lansing, Toledo, Grand Rapids the Motor City itself and finally Buffalo, I was surrounded by professional and collegiate teams that were at times at the peak of their respective sports.

The National Football League's Lions unfortunately were not able to bring home a title like their brethren the Pistons, Red Wings & Tigers during the years I covered the market. However, if the Honolulu Blue and Silver did not produce consistent winning seasons in the 1980's and 90's, they sure did produce some of the game's finest at their respective positions offensively and defensively.

I will talk about Hall of Fame running back Barry Sanders later, but a pair of his teammates also made quite a positive impression on me. Offensive Tackle Lomas Brown out of Florida and Linebacker and Ohio State product Chris Spielman to me represented what is good and right about what professional athletes should be both on and off the field.

Let's start with big Lomas. And when I say big, I mean BIG! Ok, so maybe by today's standards with lineman averaging well over 300 pounds, Brown's 6 feet 4 inch, 282 pound build might be slightly smaller. But when you shake hands with the big man or watch him try to negotiate through a normal door frame you realize you're in the presence of what I can only describe as a mobile home. And yet for all his size, Lomas was really a teddy bear off the gridiron.

During my nearly seven year stay living in suburban Detroit's West Bloomfield community, I covered each and every home Lions' game at the Pontiac Silverdome and many road contests as well. And in the magical playoff run in 1991 I was on hand for the crushing season ending loss at the hands of the host Washington Redskins at old RFK Stadium.

By the way, RFK was hands down the singularly loudest stadium I have ever been in. The stands literally bounced up and down as the home fans cheered on "The Hogs" in the midst of their glorious run as one of the NFL's best franchises.

Back to Lomas, I clearly remember the hurt in his eyes as the Lions time and again came up short for all those other seasons in terms of making it into the playoffs for a shot at the elusive Super Bowl. An optimist of the highest caliber, he honestly felt at the start of each training camp in the sweltering heat of July that come Super Bowl Sunday, he and his team-mates were a legitimate threat to be one of the participants. Ironically it wasn't until nearing the end of his career that he actually did play in the big game as a member of the New York Giants and their Super Bowl 35 loss to the Baltimore Ravens in Tampa.

It was there on the first day of media interview opportunities that I worked my way through the throng of reporters as Lomas was talking about what it was finally like to be going to play for a championship. When there was a pause in the questions I reached up on the podium he was sitting on and tapped him on his knee. Now it had been several years since we had seen each other after both of our departures from Detroit, but it was like we never left. The big guy broke into a smile and got up long enough to give me a hug and said wait until he was finished with the media questions so we could catch up briefly.

Without a doubt he was the best friend I had on the team in terms of a personal relationship. And I used that to my advantage on those many occasions that the Lions came out on the losing end of games. While many players would file by after deplaning off the club's charter or the home dressing room in the dome was anything but festive, I could always count on #75 to at least take the time for a few questions. He was a real pro and helped cement our friendship.

That leads me to a story idea I came up with involving Lomas if he would agree. Following that loss to Washington in the NFC Championship I knew he would likely tune into the Super Bowl in a couple of weeks in Minneapolis from the comfort of his living room. So here is what happened instead.

BOB & LOMAS BROWN

The story began with me nodding off on my couch and then a dream sequence visualizing the ups and downs of the just completed season concluding in D.C. I was then startled by my young sons who were shaking me awake to say that we had a guest. It turned out to be Lomas Brown stopping by to ask if he could join us to watch the game together. Needless to say the kids were thrilled and the feature concluded with all of us crowded around our new big screen television to watch as the Skins and Buffalo Bills went at it.

This was a great example of the positive personal and professional relationship we cultivated over the years. A 7 time Pro Bowl participate, he was one of the real straight shooters and I, while surprised, actually wasn't really when he revealed an incident involving a missed block while protecting (or attempting to) quarterback Scott Mitchell and the reasons behind it. I will go into more detail on that in my discussion of Mitchell coming up.

On the other side of the ball, equally as nice a guy but far more intense was Chris Spielman. I have always maintained that in the tradition of greats such as Butkus, Lambert, Nitschke & L.T., Chris was one tough son of a gun who's presence as a leader was not really appreciated on a national scale like the others mentioned.

With wins at a premium for most of his career in Detroit and the great majority of the attention on Barry Sanders, it is easy to see how that could happen. However, that is not even close to the perception we had watching him sometimes almost singlehandedly close down the offense he was facing. He was not by any means the biggest and certainly not the fastest linebacker, but for my money he was like Jack Ham of the Steelers, he was football smart. His anticipation skills were uncanny and he always, like Ham, seemed to be right in the center of activity around the ball.

His locker like that of his neighboring locker belonging to defensive lineman Marc Spindler was a perfect reflection of the man. It was always a mess and Chris always seemed to be in motion even while trying to sit and answer my questions day after day. He could get frustrated if you asked something about a particular play and he didn't believe you fully understood what was happening. I was taken to task on a few occasions, though I like to believe he knew that I knew for the most part what I was specifically talking about.

Chris has a cut on his forehead that never really healed and I am not sure if it was there when he arrived as a tough as nails rookie. But that darn thing opened up during every game he played in and always reminded me of the pro wrestling tour where many of those idiots purposely used razor blades to produce blood for their shows.

Believe me, if he could have, Spielman would have gladly caused the opposition to bleed with his take no prisoners attitude, but never to himself. He just played hard each and every play of each and every game. And if you weren't giving it all yourself, look out, because #54 had no hesitation in setting you straight.

The Lions of these years had some fine defensive talent including End Robert Porcher and Safety Bennie Blades, but there was absolutely no question who the leader of that unit was. It was Chris Spielman.

And yet for all his tough guy image and insane work ethic, Chris will likely be remembered far more for what he did off the field while temporarily giving up his career to care for his beautiful wife Stefanie who would eventually succumb to breast cancer at the age of 42.

I met Stefanie long before her initial diagnosis and she was as pretty and charming as her husband was grizzled and rough around the edges. She even did some television work of her own offering her insights into the Lions' game played earlier that day on the ABC affiliate's late evening sports segment. She was quite football savy and her perceptions were spot on.

But an eleven year battle with cancer and subsequent establishment of the Stefanie Spielman Fund for research which has raised millions of dollars for that cause, will no doubt be her and Chris's legacy.

There is a saying that goes, "A man's success has a lot to do with the kind of woman he chooses to have in his life". In the case of Chris and Stefanie Spielman that saying had a deep meaning for both parties concerned.

Lomas and Chris were men of great character and I hope Lions' fans appreciated what their considerable impact was on the franchise. No, there were no Super Bowls and to this day the team is one of only a handful of NFL teams to never even play in a Super Bowl, let alone win one.

But you need prideful, strong willed players to build a solid foundation that hopefully will outlive their own short career span on the playing field. I will always believe that Lomas Brown and Chris Spielman were two such individuals who helped lead and make those around them better players and men.

DICK BUTKUS &
GALE SAYERS

1965 was a very good year draft wise for the NFL's Chicago Bears. Right in the middle of the war with the AFL for college talent, the Bears were able to come away with not one future Hall of Famer in the first round, but a second in that same first round.

Linebacker Dick Butkus of Illinois went third overall immediately followed by running back Gale Sayers of Kansas at number four. Twenty-nine years later on a windy and rainy Halloween night at Soldier Field, both men were recognized for their on-field accomplishments by having their jersey numbers 51 and 40 respectively, retired by the organization.

Growing up in the Pittsburgh area in the 1960's my early memories of the NFL were of the Green Bay Packers on CBS with the great Ray Scott behind the microphone as well as my hometown Steelers. These were not however, the Super Steelers of today, six time Super Bowl Champions. These were the "SOS" Steelers, the Same Old Steelers of loveable owner Art Rooney who had never come close to a championship.

And then there were the Chicago Bears and the two guys that just sent shivers down my spine, albeit for completely differing reasons. The first was Butkus. Even the name sounds tough. 6 feet 3 inches and 245 pounds of snarling, in your face, rip out your throat mayhem who caused many a running back and receiver to wish he had never been born.

Talking to Dick away from the field following his retirement, he made it quite clear as he did in his Introduction for the NFL 75 Seasons book, that he was not a friend to other team's players before, during or after a game. He would chat about his meetings with the old Packers and slamming into Paul Horning and Jim Taylor, Baltimore's Lenny Moore and of course the Cleveland Browns great, Jim Brown.

DICK BUTKUS & BOB

Dick said his job was to deliver the blow to the opposition and not take it, however in Brown's case he was always tough to bring down making for quite the gridiron battle from start to finish. He especially admired Brown's decision not to run out of bounds when near the sidelines with Butkus in his sights. He felt old number 32 would have made a heckuva linebacker himself because of all the punishment he dished out.

Butkus went on after an early retirement due to multiple knee injuries to acting as well as radio broadcasting with the Bears. He has been successful in pretty much every endeavor he's attempted, but for me and most fans it's the sight of old number 51 terrorizing offenses in the 1960's and early 70's that will stand out forever.

Gale Sayers, the "Kansas Comet", the nickname from his collegiate days for the Jayhawks and maybe sadly also for how quick his comet burned out in the National Football League. Sayers became the youngest man ever enshrined in the Pro Football Hall of Fame in Canton, Ohio when he entered at just thirty-four years of age in 1977. He participated in the least amount of games of any of the Hall's members, only 68, before like Butkus his multiple knee injuries hastened his retirement.

Along with the late Roberto Clemente of my hometown Pirates, Gale was without question my all-time favorite athlete. And from being in attendance at his Hall of Fame induction to several more interview sessions in future years, it proved a wise choice because as electrifying as he was to watch on the field, Gale was every bit forthcoming as we to sat down to discuss his career highs and lows.

When we first met at the Hall I wanted him to tell me how he did what he did on the field. I mean there is no question that he was one of the greatest open field runners of his or any other generation. Cutting against the grain was his trademark and he was so unique that when he would toss a pass on the halfback option he really threw defenses off because his did so left handed. Gale could literally come to a stop then start again changing directions and it was very amusing to see defenders lose sight of him for a split second and in that split second he was gone.

Courtesy Einstein Photo

BOB & GALE SAYERS

We also discussed his well- documented friendship with running back teammate and roommate Brian Piccolo who would eventually succumb to cancer at the age of twenty-six. "Brian's Song" debuted as the ABC Movie of the Week in November of 1971 and I remember that night so clearly because less than two months earlier my father had passed away. I and my mom and younger twin sisters were all still very much in mourning. Anybody who watched that made for television film with Billy Dee Williams as Gale and James Caan as Piccolo and says they didn't shed a tear I would call a liar. At a time in my life when I was absolutely the most vulnerable emotionally, it actually helped me release much of the torment that was raging inside me. When you are a boy of fourteen and your young and seemingly healthy father (41) drops dead of a heart attack, I can tell you it confused the heck out of me and I questioned, "What does my family do now?"

Today Gale is able to look back on a very successful post football business career and he and second wife Ardie's philanthropic endeavors continue in the Chicago area. Like Butkus, he also remains a fan favorite at card shows and book signings throughout the country. Both men have a special place in my heart for the use of their talent in the game, their determination to fight back from physical and emotional trauma and most importantly their giving back to their community then as well as now. And like so many others, I simply wish their time with the Bears could have lasted longer and that they could have experienced at least one post-season game. They certainly deserved that, don't you think?

HOWARD COSELL

LIKELY nowhere in sports history has there been a man universally loved or hated more than the late former ringleader of ABC's Monday Night Football, Howard Cosell. I still have a foam brick given to me by my late mother to toss at the television after one of Cosell's ridiculous statements during the game. I always vowed if I ever got to meet him I would simply ask one question to start, "Why are you so mean?"

Well that chance came about in the summer of 1979 when I was in Las Vegas with my mom as a gift from her to me for graduation from Ohio University. We were not staying at Caesars' Palace on the Strip, but I knew that night Sugar Ray Leonard and Tony Chiaverini were about to fight in an NABF Welterweight showdown and that Cosell would be calling the action for ABC. I purposely brought with me my tape recorder and microphone and sure enough late that morning of the bout there was Cosell sitting poolside with Caesar's Marketing Director at the time Bob Halloran.

I timidly approached Howard who surprisingly was polite enough to introduce me to Halloran and then simply asked, "What is it that I can do for you young man?" I quickly advised him of my desire to get a taped interview to give to my college radio station and again I was fairly shocked to have him agree, though there was the hint of a huff in his voice.

The interview lasted approximately 15 minutes with my first question out of the gate regarding how I might begin my quest to get into the business. Cosell bombastically began, "Don't even try. The broadcast medium has corrupted itself by hiring totally unqualified people as a measure of cheap expediency. What there should be in sports broadcasting in America are properly trained young people in the fields of communications and journalism who should be working as you're working, getting training at the local radio station. Instead the broadcast medium has elected to put on anybody who threw a ball or caught a ball if they were proficient enough at that to get national attention.

One of the tragedies in what broadcasters have done by hiring jocks is to dilute and distill the hopes and dreams of young people properly prepared in the fields of journalism. In television there are no heroes there are no villains there are only ratings and you must learn this young man. Anyone who says otherwise is lying to themselves or to others"

And as far as his move from law to the broadcast industry he responded, "There happened to be a broadcast opportunity thru one of my clients. I never dreamed it would be in sports. I would have much preferred to have been in national or international news, more in keeping with my intellect and my need for intellectual challenges. It happened to be in sports and sports at the time had absolutely no journalism. I became THE sports journalist in broadcasting, willing to tell the truth, willing to deal with broad issues that people never think about."

Finally I was absolutely shocked with Cosell's response to my next question regarding possible friendships developed over the years with some of the "jocks" he talked about each week such as Sugar Ray Leonard. Clearly from the time Leonard burst on the scene at the 1976 Olympics in Montreal, Howard was all over the coverage and lauding to whomever would listen the strengths and character of the young boxer.

Yet when I asked if he had a personal relationship with Ray away from the cameras and the ring, he responded, "I like Sugar Ray Leonard. The victory of our Olympic boxing team at Montreal was a triumph of the human spirit. But Sugar Ray Leonard isn't equipped by educational background or anything else to be a personal friend of mine. No."

Wow! That's all I can say. I just wish in the several meetings I had with Leonard over the years I would have relayed this information to him. I believe he would be hurt and likely taken aback by Howard's abrupt kiss off. But then again Howard's dead and what's done is done.

I do think from some of these answers given to a cub reporter you get a good idea what Howard Cosell was all about and his moniker of "Tell it like it is" was well earned. I am usually a pretty good judge of character and I was pleased to find that my impressions from Howard on television were in fact what the man was really like. He didn't seem happy at all with his position which is sad because not being able to be in broadcasting today as I once was I miss the rush of adrenaline it provided. But I did get the chance to speak with the mouth that roared and Howard Cosell did not disappoint.

MIKE DITKA

"**IRON**" Mike Ditka is easily the most intense person I've ever interviewed. He just always seemed wound up when we spoke. Whether it was regarding his playing and coaching career or even when we were at the golf tournament bearing his name in the town he was raised in of Aliquippa, Pennsylvania.

From his humble beginnings in Western PA to the face you regularly saw on ESPN and continue to see in commercials, Ditka always speaks his mind and if you don't like what he says that's too bad. Fair, but firm is the best way to describe him. And it is not hard to see where he got his personality traits from.

His late mother Charlotte was quite a gal herself. A few years ago while playing in the Ditka golf outing, I was coming up the 9th fairway after chipping my shot to the green. Admittedly it wasn't my best hole and Mrs. Ditka was quick to point that out. She hollered over to me, "Young man, don't play a lot of golf do you? I was embarrassed, but at the same time had to giggle a bit because she was so into what was going on and having fun with everybody. I came over and gave her a quick hug before putting and said to her, "I appreciate you noticing me and thank you for taking the time to say hello in your own special way." She got a good laugh too from her lawn chair perched at the back of the green.

Meanwhile Mike himself is just one tough cookie. He's one of only two men to have won Super Bowls as a player, an assistant coach and a head coach and the only man to have been a part of the Chicago Bears last two World Championships. He was a tight end on the 1963 team coached by the legendary George "Papa Bear" Halas and of course was the Head Coach when Chicago captured Super Bowl XX in 1985.

MIKE DITKA & BOB

What I like about Ditka again is his overall intensity and passion. I've always told my own sons that is what separates successful people from unsuccessful people. You must have a passion in your life and football is definitely "Iron" Mike's. You also have to be true to your heart in decision making and there's little doubt that right or wrong, he goes with his gut instinct.

A classic example is the draft he had with the New Orleans Saints in 1999. There he traded away all of the club's eight choices along with the first selection in 2000 for the right to move up and take University of Texas running back and Heisman Trophy winner Ricky Williams. Even though the retired Williams did become the twenty-sixth player in history to rush for over 10,000 career yards, he did not help bring the Saints a title and the draft fiasco eventually cost Ditka his job. Ricky later moved on to Miami and finally Baltimore before retiring in 2012.

There is however, no arguing with his overall success. A five time Pro Bowler as a player, a three time Super Bowl champion and an NFL Hall of Fame selection in 1988, where he became the hall's first tight end ever enshrined. He set the bar to which all future players at that position are compared.

TONY DORSETT

ANOTHER Beaver County native who was an exceptional athlete in his day is former running back Tony Dorsett, the pride of Hopewell High School. Tony was three years ahead of me while I toiled at Center High School in the neighboring community of Center Township. As a matter of fact, in 2011, Center merged with another neighboring town, Monaca, to create the new Central Valley school district which has among other things, developed into a state powerhouse athletically in both boys and girls sports.

In his senior season with the Vikings in 1972, Tony was one of the more highly recruited players in the eastern half of the country and there was little doubt that whatever college he chose to take his considerable talents to, he would make an impact. Turns out he needed go no farther than approximately 30 miles to the southeast to Pittsburgh and the lowly Panthers.

Following a one win season and the firing of head coach Carl DePasqua, Pitt made the fortuitous choice to replace DePasqua with 1956 Heisman Trophy runner-up, Johnny Majors from Tennessee. From that point on, Dorsett and Majors would forever be linked together because in just four short seasons, the Panthers went from a single victory to an undefeated record and the National Championship after knocking off Georgia in the 1977 Sugar Bowl in New Orleans.

Dorsett and Majors put Pitt on the football map as a destination for some of the most outstanding talent on both sides of the football from that point forward. During the 70's, 80's and 90's the school produced NFL Hall of Famers such as Dorsett, Dan Marino, Ricky Jackson and Curtis Martin. Many other future pros came through Pitt including the single finest all-around defensive player I ever witnessed in college, Hugh Green, along with some incredibly gifted offensive lineman, names like Jimbo Covert, Bill Fralic, Russ Grimm and Mark May among them.

But it was "T.D." who began that trend as he started as a freshman, ironically against those same Bulldogs of Vince Dooley that he would eventually face in his final game on a much bigger national stage. He set the NCAA record for yards rushing by a freshman with 1,586, became Pittsburgh's all-time rushing leader in only his sophomore year and when he was finished, held the all-time Division 1 mark in rushing yardage with 6,082 while winning the Heisman Trophy.

Not too shabby for a skinny little kid from Aliquippa who soaking wet might have weighed 157 pounds as a high school senior. But he could run and over the next four years packed on muscle without losing any of his speed or acceleration.

When he became the first round draft choice of the Dallas Cowboys, he was a chiseled 192 pounds and the rest is history. NFL Rookie of the Year and Super Bowl XII champion (the only player EVER to be a part of a college national championship team one year and Super Bowl winner the next). As of this writing, he stands eighth all-time in the list of professional football running backs with 12,739 yards and 90 total touchdowns (77 rushing and 13 receiving).

But to those who saw his grace and ability to dash and dart through defenses, Tony Dorsett was much more than statistics. He simply seemed to glide with a casual effortlessness the belied really how quickly he was moving. Much like Gale Sayers before him and Barry Sanders afterwards, Dorsett was always a man in motion with a smile on his face, but a deadly serious determination to break free. Funny to think that like an unbroken stallion, Tony's two pro teams were the Cowboys and the Broncos.

I have spoken with him during my pre-broadcasting days at one of Pitt's favorite hangouts, Peter's Pub, in the Oakland section of Pittsburgh near the university campus. Then later as a professional at the Hall of Fame in Canton where he was enshrined in 1994 and various memorabilia shows.

BOB & TONY DORSETT

As flashy as he was on the field though, he was never a real fan of media types like myself. Fortunately reminding him of our close proximity growing up in Western Pennsylvania made our recorded conversations a better experience than most got out of him. He was misunderstood as being aloof, when in fact he was really just shy more than anything and quite thoughtful in his answers when he did speak. Nothing wrong with that in my eyes, I mean, not everybody can be as comfortable with a camera in their face as Sparky or Iron Mike. For Dorsett it was a battle at times.

These days, his battle is of a more serious nature with his announcement in 2013 that he is suffering mentally with memory loss as well as personality issues. He has been diagnosed with CTE or Chronic Traumatic Encephalopathy. It is a brain disease that has been discovered by doctors found in football players and boxers primarily from repeated blows to the head. Sadly only recently has the NFL finally admitted after years and years of constant denials, that in fact head trauma caused by contact time and again IS a major contributor to former athletes now in a debilitated state far from the spotlight.

Several of Dorsett's contemporaries have taken the drastic step of suicide to end their own suffering. Chicago Bears' defensive back and Super Bowl XX champ Dave Duerson and 2015 Hall of Fame linebacker Junior Seau, just two of several prominent players who shot themselves to death in the chest. These were unfortunate, but nonetheless premeditated acts. And that premeditation is proof that these men knew exactly what they were doing, but at the same time leaving the tissue necessary and intact to study post-mortem. Even prior to his own symptoms developing, Tony was very active in reaching out to current and former NFL players with health issues related to their playing days.

My memories, however, are very clear of watching a young Tony Dorsett and his run towards football greatness. And for you trivia buffs, of the thousands upon thousands of NCAA and NFL players in history, only Tony and fellow running back Marcus Allen have the distinction of winning the Heisman Trophy, a College National Championship, NFL Rookie of the Year, the Super Bowl and are members of both the College and Pro Football Halls of Fame.

JOE DUMARS &
ISIAH THOMAS

THE Detroit Pistons won back to back NBA Championships in the 1988-89 and 1989-90 seasons and were nicknamed the "Bad Boys" because of their rough and tumble style of play. Center Bill Laimbeer and Forward Rick Mahorn led that style, but honestly the heart and soul of those teams were the guards, Joe Dumars and Captain Isiah Thomas.

During my stay in Detroit I spoke regularly with both men and got insights into what it takes not only to become a champion in a particular sport, but to stay there when the rest of the league wants to knock you down. All players will tell you when you are in defense of a title the opposition always comes at you with their "A" game. There are really no nights off even during an arduous eighty game schedule and then hopefully the playoffs.

Dumars and Thomas were silky smooth, but underlying that smoothness was a killer instinct, a passionate focus that drove these men to heights they and their team only dreamed of and eventually each to the National Basketball Hall of Fame.

Let's start with Joe D. Drafted number one in 1985 out of Louisiana's McNeese State, he teamed with Thomas to complete one of the best backcourts the NBA has ever produced. Initially a shooting guard while Thomas held down the point, Dumars moved to point guard in 1994 following Isiah's retirement and then teamed with another number one draft choice, Duke's Grant Hill, until Joe's retirement in after fourteen seasons in 1999.

Unlike the effervescent Thomas, Joe was a much quieter personality, but certainly no less intense on the court. Yet that gentlemanly style of play did earn him the NBA's first ever Sportsmanship award in 1996 and that trophy is now named in his honor. Joe stepped down from his role as President of the Pistons immediately after the 2014 regular season ended, but still operates the Joe Dumars Fieldhouse in Shelby Township, Michigan, considered Detroit's premier league sports and events center.

Over my years in Detroit we spoke often about basketball, but my main memory of Joe was his personal interest in how I was doing in the midst of my mom's failing health and eventual passing in the spring of 1995. Joe was most comforting and caring as it turned out that his own mother was ill and died not long after my mother did. These are the kinds of things that stand out in my mind when I speak of certain athletes and their personalities. Joe was a good friend at that time and I will always remember his sincerity regarding my situation at home.

Then there's Isiah. Man could that young man run an offense. Thomas brought grit to the position and determination that made him go after much bigger men than himself in the game. Like Joe D., Thomas was a number one draft selection as well going second overall in 1981. He was named one of the NBA's Top 50 players and retired after 13 seasons in 1994.

BOB & ISIAH THOMAS

That huge scar above his left eye is courtesy of Utah's "Mailman", the 6 foot 9 inch muscular Karl Malone who just crushed Isiah during a game when he was driving for a lay-up. The bone jarring hit would have put most players in the dressing room, but not Isiah who kept playing. He would have more than his share of run-ins with opponents such as Michael Jordan, but at the same time had great relationships with others including "Magic" Johnson, both of whom I will talk about later.

Thomas moved to become the Head Coach at Florida International University after stints in the NBA as Head Coach for Indiana as well as the New York Knicks. He's always been a driven personality and one known for his fashion statements as well. I always appreciated his comments to me when he saw me regarding my choice of suits or shirts and ties. For the millions of dollars less I made compared to him, I always thought his words were a real compliment.

Both Joe and Isiah helped put the Pistons on the map and it is their legacy that the franchise must follow. Hard work, dedication, selflessness and commitment were the keys to their on the court success and continue to be so in their post playing days.

THE "FAB FIVE"

COINCIDING with the professional basketball success of the Pistons, was that of the nearby University of Michigan. National Champs in 1989 following a thrilling overtime title game in Seattle against St. John's, the Wolverines did so in the midst of some very unusual circumstances.

The 1988-89 season began under the direction of Head Coach Bill Frieder who had been at the helm of the program since 1980. But as March Madness was about to get underway with the start of the NCAA Tournament, word got out that Frieder had a verbal agreement to take over as head coach at Arizona State after the season ended. New U of M Athletic Director and legendary football Head Coach Bo Schembechler wasted no time in putting a premature end to Bill's Wolverine coaching days. Bo immediately fired him and promoted assistant Steve Fisher to lead the team into the tourney. His now famous line that, "A Michigan man will coach Michigan!" still resonates strongly with me.

And all Fisher did was lead the maize and blue to six consecutive tournament victories including that dramatic overtime win to wrap up the championship. It was a situation that could have created understandable blowback and seriously threaten what had been a superb 24 win regular season. But Michigan never missed a beat and a lot of that had to do with the calm presence of Steve Fisher.

He remains the only coach in the history of the game to win an NCAA National Championship without ever having lost a single game during the regular season because he wasn't the head coach. Think about that. Fisher had been a career college assistant coach to that point in time.

Fast forward to 1991 and the affable head coach and his staff recruited the most recognized and significant freshman class in the history of collegiate hoops. "The Fab Five" as they quickly became known were made up of Chris Webber, Jalen Rose, Juwan Howard, Jimmy King and Ray Jackson. And they became the first ever all freshmen squad to start an NCAA game when they did so against Notre Dame in February of 1992.

From that point until the end of their second consecutive National Championship game loss to North Carolina as sophomores in April of 1993, there were no more recognizable or controversial players in all of college basketball.

Likewise I arrived in Detroit in the fall of 1991 and among my duties at WKBD-TV saw many days and evenings spent in Ann Arbor at Crisler Arena (now named Crisler Center) for practices and games featuring this growing cultural phenomenon. First and foremost for me, they were fun to be around and highly entertaining off the court as well as on. From their baggy shorts, black shoes and socks, shaved heads and a swagger and confidence I had never seen in such young college athletes, you just could not help but be drawn to them.

These kids from Detroit, Chicago, Austin and Plano, Texas clicked almost from the time they arrived on campus and as far as I am concerned the game of college basketball was forever changed. "Trash Talking" was taken to a whole new level by this band of brothers who's mix of wide open street ball combined with what Steve Fisher was trying to do with the x's and o's produced a new style all their own.

Running and gunning, tenacious defensive pressure all the while playing a game above the rim, "The Fab Five" made it must see viewing in person and on television from coast to coast for two fabulous seasons. Then after the heartbreak and public humiliation Webber faced following his ill- fated "time out" call in the Louisiana Superdome in the waning seconds of the Tar Heels' loss, Chris decided to leave for the NBA. Jalen and Juwan followed the next year and that was that.

In between, their freshman year was capped by a trip to the Final Four in Minneapolis where they would fall in the title matchup against the Christian Laettner led Duke Blue Devils. From my seat on press row inside the Metrodome I watched the kids lead by a point at the half, but eventually break down and go on to lose by twenty.

And just as he would do a year later in New Orleans, Webber stormed past the gathered media horde in the tunnel including our cameras, and went into a profanity laced tirade before settling down to join his coach and teammates at the podium for the obligatory "post- game press conference".

Chris and Jalen more than the others were very emotional outwardly and it worked both for and against them at times. Jimmy was pretty brash as well, Juwan was the steadiest of the brood as the big man in the middle and Ray was pretty quiet. Yet when Howard and Jackson spoke, it had meaning and everybody listened.

Sadly, after my departure for the EMPIRE Sports Network, a pair of investigations resulted in all mention of "The Fab Five" and their collective accomplishments be stricken from the official record. A booster by the name of Ed Martin had infiltrated the inner circle with not only Webber charged with accepting cash and other illegal contributions from Martin, but several other prominent Wolverine players in future years as well.

So the banners that once hung proudly inside Crisler are packed away and those exciting days of "The Fab Five" dominating the Big Ten and beyond are long since over. But those of us that were there can still look back fondly on that brief shining moment of basketball "Camelot" in Ann Arbor when five kids introduced us to their unique collective talents. And it makes me smile.

WAYNE FONTES

A coaching personality that I spent many hours with during my tenure in Detroit and will never forget is Wayne Fontes. He was primarily a defensive assistant when he was hired to lead the Detroit Lions in 1988 and during his reign, guided the Lions to the playoffs four times, most impressively the first time in 1991 making it all the way to the NFC Championship game at Washington.

Wayne was a good guy and I hosted his coach's show on WKBD-TV on Sunday night's following games. But I always felt he was trying to do too much or be somebody he wasn't. He took the role as head coach and did some crazy things like drive around training camp and regular season practices much like Mike Ditka did in a floppy hat and golf cart. He was a character that morphed into a "caricature" of himself and I wonder if at times his players didn't see that as well.

We got along and I'd like to think I got to know him quite well over the years. I thoroughly enjoyed speaking with him and getting him to toss out some of his famous observations. One such time was on the show following a comeback win on the road. I asked the coach what turned things around and he in all seriousness said, "Bob, it was a game of two halves." I almost burst out laughing on "live" television because he was dead serious, but it just sounded so corny at the time.

WAYNE FONTES & BOB

His personnel decisions were strong and when you look back at those years you wonder why this team didn't win more or advance in the playoffs farther. I mean you had one of the finest running backs in history in Barry Sanders from 1989 on plus a tenacious defense led by strong safety Bennie Blades and linebacker Chris Spielman. The main problem, however, was Fontes' decisions at quarterback.

The Lions had Rodney Peete as their starter in 1991, the former 6th round pick out of USC. But Rodney suffered a season ending injury in game number three and was replaced by Erik Kramer. Kramer started the remaining thirteen games and led Detroit to a 12 and 4 record and the team's first post-season appearance since 1957. "The Roar was Restored" in Motown. Detroit then buried Jimmy Johnson and a young Cowboys team that included Troy Aikman, Michael Irvin, and Emmitt Smith at home before failing miserably against the eventual Super Bowl champion Redskins in the NFC Championship at RFK Stadium.

Now Kramer had performed far better than anyone had expected and based upon that performance many observers (including myself) believed he deserved to enter training camp in 1992 as the starter, or at the very least get to compete for the job. Fontes did not agree. His philosophy was a player could not lose his position due to injury so when camp opened Peete was reinstalled as the starter.

Kramer was devastated and was never the same player again for Detroit because he felt Wayne betrayed him. He had good reason to be upset. To that point no Lions' team had advanced to the playoffs since the late 1950's and as of today, no Lions' team has ever made it as far as the NFC Championship contest.

That victory over the Dallas in the 1991 playoffs was the last in the post-season for Detroit. Even more troubling to me in 2015 was the news that Erik, a very cooperative and engaging man with ever growing confidence during that 1991 season, had attempted suicide. He survived that attempt, but his ex-wife described him as severely depressed following his playing days and that repeated head trauma was the suspected cause.

Overall again I feel Wayne was a good coach and tried to get the most out of his players, but by the end again he was that "caricature" called "Big Buck", named after his perceived lack of job security and a target on his back like a deer.

As an irony to sum up Wayne Fontes' career, no Lions coach ever won more games or lost more games than he did.

TERRY FRANCONA

I always take great pride when speaking about success stories from athletes here in Western Pennsylvania.. Former Philadelphia Phillies and Boston Red Sox manager, and now skipper of the Cleveland Indians, Terry Francona sure fits that bill. Terry was a year behind me in high school in Beaver County as I attended Center and he went to New Brighton where his father, former major leaguer John "Tito" Francona attended in the 1940's. My mom in fact was a member of that same graduating class as "Tito".

Terry, who's also known by the nickname "Tito", went on to star at the University of Arizona and was the 1980 College Player of the Year. He then was drafted by the Montreal Expos in the first round as an outfielder then first baseman, but injuries primarily to his knees stalled his career as an active player after nine seasons and five teams and he decided to go into coaching.

He made it back to the major league level as a third base coach with Buddy Bell's Detroit Tigers in 1996 after a minor league coaching and managerial career that included skippering Michael Jordan in 1994 with the Birmingham Barons.

That's where I first caught back up with him on a professional level as my assignment with WKBD-TV was to cover the first week of spring training each baseball season. I found Terry to be as warm and friendly as he was back in his high school days, but under his quiet exterior he was a bulldog for perfection and demanded as such from his players.

We spoke about home and his rise to the major leagues as a player and then coach and his desire to one day manage his own ballclub. Francona was and is one of those people who knows exactly what he wants and more importantly how to get there.

Courtesy Bill Eisner

BOB & TERRY FRANCONA

So after his short one year stint in Detroit he was offered the Phillies managerial spot in 1997 at the age of 38. He had a four year run with Philadelphia before being fired after the 2000 season. He had a couple of seasons as a bench coach with both Texas and Oakland before being offered to manage the Red Sox and what a ride that was.

Eleven years guiding Boston produced World Series crowns in his first season of 2004, then three years later again in 2007. The "Curse of the Bambino" lifted, Terry and his players became household names around the country.

Unfortunately all good things must end and he was relieved of his duties at the end of the 2011 season after the Sox blew a nine game divisional lead to Tampa Bay as part of a miserable 7-20 month of September to miss the playoffs altogether.

But Terry will always have that magical season of 2004 when the

Boston Red Sox at long last captured their first title since 1919. As the wild card entry, Boston came back from a three games to none deficit in the American League Championship Series over the hated Yankees then dispatched St. Louis almost as an afterthought 4-0 to win the World Series.

He exemplifies the traits that go into the making of a winner. He is always focused and prepared. There are no excuses. He also is smart enough to surround himself with like-minded individuals who help carry out his mantra. If you check out his track record, his methods are really hard to argue with.

Following one season as an expert commentator for ESPN, Terry is back doing what he was born to do and that's manage a big league ballclub with the Cleveland Indians. And those of us in Beaver County remain proud not only of Terry Francona's accomplishments, but the way in which he conducts himself on a daily basis.

STEVE GARVEY &
TOM LASORDA

IN the foreward to this book I spoke of my first experience gaining a "press pass" and meeting with Los Angeles Dodgers' skipper Tom Lasorda. Well there's more to that story and it involves 10 time all-star first baseman Steve Garvey.

As I mentioned, I was all set to go credential wise at Three Rivers Stadium for interviews with both the Dodgers and Pirates, but I truly didn't know that process yet and what I did cannot happen in today's sports landscape. Or at least it shouldn't if team media officials have their way. I called Lasorda's room from the lobby of Pittsburgh's Hilton Hotel and was amazed to find he actually answered that call and advised me to wait in the lobby as he would be right down.

What a thrill it was as he extended his hand and asked how I was getting to the stadium. I told him I had my car parked downstairs in the hotel garage. He invited me to ride the short distance across the bridge to Three Rivers on the team bus. I went along with the suggestion and could not believe my good fortune. He said just sit anywhere and we'd get together inside his dressing room office once we arrived.

Now understand this, I was a 19 year old college sophomore and while I am quite outgoing, this was a bit unnerving. I mean where do you sit on a team bus with names like Garvey, Cey, Russell and Lopes? Who's foot would I be stepping on, who's window seat? Well common sense advised going towards the back and that's what I did, just two rows from the back of the bus. I slid over to the window, crouched down and started looking over some notes on questions I'd like to ask Lasorda.

Within a few moments a voice I immediately recognized asked, "Is this seat taken?" It was none other than Steve Garvey. I was honestly shaking in my shoes when he sat down in the aisle seat and introduced himself, "Steve

Garvey, what's your name?" Yes I had a brain fart moment and almost forgot not only where I was, but who I was. I finally meekly offered, "Bob Trimble Mr. Garvey, Ohio University and the All Campus Radio Network." "Nice to meet you Bob, please call me Steve and I see you've already met Tommy. So what brings you here today?"

I went on to explain this was my first professional encounter with a team and that Lasorda was nice enough to let me tag along. At the time Garvey had just signed a new monster $330,000 per year deal with L.A. and I asked if I could speak with him once inside as well and he readily agreed.

The bus just then pulled up at the stadium and there must have been thirty to forty fans waiting to say hello and get some autographs. As we got off the bus Steve went right to the fans as did many of the Dodger players and he said, "Bob, come on over and sign some baseballs." So I did and to this day have to have a laugh when I think of folks in that area bringing home baseballs signed Steve Garvey, Tom Lasorda and, Bob Trimble? That just cracks me up every time I think about it and Steve I know got a great laugh out of it as well.

TOM LASORDA & BOB AT SPRING TRAINING IN LAKELAND, FL

The skipper was true to his word inviting me into his small office as soon as I got in and we spoke for a good half an hour. It was at that time I first heard the phrase, "I bleed Dodger blue" and Tommy was almost nonstop in his praise of the organization and for it giving him the opportunity to manage this storied franchise. "I've been entrusted by the owners to continue to win and bring championships to Southern California.". Lasorda took over the reins from longtime skipper Walter Alston who had managed the club since its days in Brooklyn.

Once our session was over Lasorda called out to an equipment man and said get me a brand new baseball for Bobby here. He signed his name perfectly on the sweet spot and advised I go around the dressing room and get the whole team to sign it as a keepsake of my visit. What a wonderful and unforgettable gesture on the part of Tommy.

I then went over to Steve and we spoke and then on to the rest of the team for those autographs. I later learned this practice of a reporter getting an autograph especially inside the dressing room with accredited access is frowned upon to the point of if you are found doing so, your credential can and likely will be revoked and you'd be asked to leave the stadium. But that was not the case on this day in this situation thanks to Tom Lasorda and Steve Garvey. They helped make my first press credentialed game one of the main reasons I wanted more of it in the future.

BOB & STEVE GARVEY

Years later at the 1984 World Series in Detroit I got to say high to Steve again, this time as a member of the San Diego Padres. Though he did not immediately remember me, once I began the story of the bus ride and the autographs with the fans he broke into a wide grin and said, "Yeah Bob I DO remember that day."

I will always remember it too Steve. You and your manager made my first day utilizing my "press pass" one of the best!

KIRK GIBSON &
BILL LAIMBEER

IN the 1980's and 90's the Detroit sports scene was one of winners when speaking about the city's pro sports franchises. The Tigers won the 1984 World Series, the Pistons captured back to back NBA Championships in 1988 and 89 and the Red Wings won hockey's Stanley Cup in 1996 and 97.

Two of the names featured on those first two titles were baseball's Kirk Gibson and basketball's Bill Laimbeer. Gibby was by far the more naturally gifted athlete having been a three sport star in high school in suburban Detroit and a talented, physical receiver at Michigan State. Laimbeer was more of a workhorse big and strong, but not fleet of foot. He used a physical presence like Gibson as well as an under your skin irritating attitude to get the most out of himself and the teammates around him.

Truth be told, neither of these guys were particularly friendly especially during their respective seasons. For instance my first trip to the Palace of Auburn Hills which is home to the Pistons was less than memorable as a member of the media. Following a rare Detroit home loss I was the first media member that walked into the modern, yet still somewhat cramped dressing room area and who was there to greet me, but Laimbeer. The quote was, "Yeah, so who are you and what do you want?" I responded, "I'm Bob Trimble from WKBD-TV and I'm here to get some post-game comments". "Well do I care?" offered big Bill who simply turned and walked to the shower and never to be seen again, at least by me that evening.

Years later at his retirement ceremony in that same Palace of Auburn Hills I reminded Laimbeer of his less than cordial greeting to me in my first week on the job and he laughed. He said had he not actually known of me he would not have put me through that awkward moment. He'd seen me on the air and just wanted to rattle my cage a little to see how I reacted. We never really had any issues after that, though Bill was intense to a fault and did make it uncomfortable at times to get him to talk.

Gibson was flat out moody and depending on his mood you either got a sound bite for the ages or simply a cold shoulder and I experienced both. He was clearly the team leader and his heroics in the 1984 World Series against San Diego are stuff of dreams, with two home runs in game 5 at home to secure the title. He was one of those rare athletes who had the ability to rise to the occasion when needed.

Four years later his limp to the plate and ensuing homer off the A's Dennis Eckersley is now one of the top moments in baseball history as he helped propel the Dodgers to another World Series championship.

On that negative side, however, I watched in horror as he blew off a little girl asking for an autograph following a Tigers' workout in Lakeland, Florida in Spring Training one year. I'd seen this before with men and crowds, but at this particular moment there might have been ten people around and this girl could not have been more than nine or ten years of age.

As the hulking Gibson waded past her the look on her face made me just shake my head in disgust. I could in no way help her, but fortunately shortstop Alan Trammell was close behind and he gladly stopped to sign for her and the others. Tram was a beauty to deal with.

Just like Laimbeer, when Gibby retired there was a big shindig. The retirement was coupled with the release of a coffee table style book recounting Gibson's rise from high school through college and then the major leagues. On that night he could not have been more outgoing & friendly to all in attendance, including those of us in the media. I just wish he had been so a little more often to the media and especially that little girl in Lakeland.

Today Kirk Gibson is suffering from Parkinson's Syndrome and I do personally feel bad for a man who's physical gifts he utilized to their max. He epitomized to me a win at all costs approach and did nothing but hustle. But now the body he threw around day after day and night after night to reach that goal is unfortunately breaking down at far too young an age.

WAYNE GRETZKY

AS a Pittsburgh area native I grew up with "The Great One", Pirates Hall of Fame right fielder Roberto Clemente. But to the rest of the sporting world "The Great One" played hockey and his name was Wayne Gretzky.

For twenty seasons he dominated the National Hockey League like no other player before or since setting records likely never to be broken. He is the NHL's all-time point leader, nine times the league MVP, ten times its leading scorer and the only man ever to tally 200 points in a single season (he actually did it four different times). And he was a heckuva nice guy all the while, capturing the Lady Byng Trophy for sportsmanship another five times.

I spoke to Wayne many times following regular season and playoff games, an All-Star game weekend in Pittsburgh and when he put together his own group of all-stars on tour during the 1995 lockout. I found him to have no ego whatsoever and as genuine a person as I'd ever met.

Wayne is generally regarded as the greatest hockey player in history and his statistics add credence to that claim. Having seen him play in person and on television hundreds of times I must admit I agree. However, had Pittsburgh's Mario Lemieux not gone through a myriad of injuries and illnesses he would be right alongside of Gretzky in the conversation.

What I liked about Wayne on the ice was the smoothness and flow to his game. Experts always point to a player who sees the game in a kind of "slow motion" and that certainly was this guy. Wayne was able to see avenues for a pass or shot that were two to three moves ahead in the fast paced action. His was an incredible gift to make other professionals look to be mere mortal as he seemed to effortlessly skate circles around them on the way to yet another scoring play.

When I spent the most time with Wayne during the lockout all-star tour we spoke about his beginnings in Brantford, Ontario. It is a fact, he was just head and shoulders above others in the talent department while much younger and smaller. Gretzky was without question the finest player from the time he took to the ice in his backyard and proved it time and again with grace and style.

I was always amazed at hockey players in general and how in between periods of actual games they take time to speak "live" with a member of the broadcast crew to get their impressions of play to that point.

I wonder in twenty years as a professional how many times Wayne Gretzky took time to do just that? And while I don't have an answer for that question I do know that "The Great One" was every bit that and more in each and every one of our interview sessions.

GORDIE HOWE

WHILE Wayne Gretzky is considered to be the greatest hockey player in NHL history, the man who revolutionized the sport and played a physical game Gretzky never did was his idol "Mr. Hockey", Gordie Howe.

Howe played professionally in parts of six different decades and until Wayne came along held every major offensive record including total points, goals and assists. All that while using his Popeye style forearms and elbows to keep the opposition at bay and in check.

I probably had the best relationship with Gordie of any of the thousands of interview subjects I had during my broadcast career. We first met in 1982 at the Battle Creek, Michigan World Hockey Tournament where Howe was in attendance to promote the event between teams representing Canada, China, Japan and the United States. Gordie's presence ensured solid attendance and in fact he was more popular than the players and teams taking part in the tourney.

Over the next twenty plus years we got together numerous times whether it be another appearance promoting the sport he loved, one of my "One on One sports challenges, numerous charity golf events or celebrating his return to the game in 1997. That was for a one game contract with the International Hockey League's Detroit Vipers. Let's go into detail on two of those meetings.

GORDIE HOWE & BOB

First, my "One on One" fan participation series was going great guns on a weekly basis for WZZM-TV in Grand Rapids, Michigan when it was proposed that we get Gordie involved. He came to Muskegon for an autograph appearance & would then suit up in his late 50's and take a handful of penalty shots on a goaltender between periods of the Lumberjacks' minor league home game. That goalie would be, you guessed it, Bob Trimble.

I honestly love hockey, I just never played it because I was a very weak skater. But I thought what the heck, how much skating will I have to do in net? And Gordie was a real pro advising me to simply get in position he'd do the rest. How embarrassing then when we got out on the ice and I felt like I was in a suit of armor, heavy armor.

How do goalies do it? I mean how do they move so freely in this stuff? Now I'm no weakling, but I sure felt like one and stupid too since Mr. Hockey had to skate up and properly tie my skate laces which had come undone. While there Gordie asked, "Are you ready Bobby?" I nodded and he added, "Keep an eye out for number three, ok?" He then winked at me and skated away to center ice for the first of the five penalty shots.

As he came slowly towards me on the first attempt I know I had a bladder issue just as his wrist shot hit me in the right shoulder and harmlessly fell away from the net. I BLOCKED IT! No not really, I just happened to get hit where I stood because I didn't and couldn't move.

Number two was another wristed effort, this time low to the left and it hit the twine easily. So we're one apiece and here he comes with number three, THWACK, right in the face off my mask. Yes I did urinate then. It didn't hurt, but I was so slow reacting I couldn't believe it.

BOB & GORDIE

I really don't even remember shots four and five because I just wanted to sit down. Five minutes on the ice and I was exhausted and dripping sweat. Gordie warmly skated off with me and knowing of my sports memorabilia collection gave me the jersey and stick he used, signing both, "To Bobby, In Friendship, Gordon Howe". What a thrill even if I was embarrassed by my performance.

Moving forward to 1997 now at age sixty-nine Gordie suited up for that one game contract with the Vipers of the International Hockey League. Interestingly the late Colleen Howe, Gordie's wife and manager asked me the best location and time for a press conference to announce the event. Imagine that, me getting asked what would be the best time and place. I thanked Colleen because it is usually the other way around and I've never forgotten her kindness. Fortunately nobody on visiting Kansas City's roster decided to take a run at Gordo during his single shift and the evening went off beautifully.

From the 1940's to the 50's, 60's, 70's, 80's and finally the 90's, Gordie Howe was a star like no other in his sport and he will always be the biggest star in my book for the time he took to speak with me. He was a true gentleman. Today's athletes could take a few tips from "Mr. Hockey" on how to treat fans and media alike.

His passing just 8 days following that of Muhammad Ali in June of 2016 left me as saddened as I was being informed of my own father's death. But I also felt truly blessed that I was able to spend some incredible times with two of the most important and transcendent figures of this or any other lifetime.

THOMAS HEARNS &
"SUGAR" RAY LEONARD

BOXING was always one of my favorite sports made even more so once I had the chance to meet and interview some of its stars. We've already discussed Muhammad Ali so now it's time to talk about a pair of fighters outside the heavyweight division, but true heavyweights when it comes to star power.

Thomas "The Hit Man" Hearns and Sugar Ray Leonard were dominating forces in the 1980's and 90's. Tommy in fact fought in six different weight divisions during his career, Leonard in five. Versatile, talented athletes, both men made boxing exciting to watch and their matches were two of the most anticipated and viewed in history.

Hearns came up through the ranks as an amateur and Golden Gloves champ while Sugar Ray made his name as an undefeated U.S. Olympic Light Welterweight champion in 1976 in Montreal. He too won multiple Golden Gloves amateur titles.

In their first fight dubbed "The Showdown" in 1981 to unify the World Welterweight division, Leonard was able to pull off a late rally and defeat Tommy as the fight was stopped in the 14th round. But it was not until 1989 that the rivals were able to get their much ballyhooed rematch once again at Caesar's Palace in Las Vegas. It was on their pre-fight press tour that I first got to meet Hearns and Leonard in Grand Rapids.

Dapper and ever so smooth, both men went through the paces of my questions with ease having been grilled over the years by national media types far more experienced in their individual backgrounds and that of the sport itself. Yet when complete, Tommy and Ray each thanked me for taking the time to sit down and said if I requested a credential to please advise their public relations representatives to say hello.

THOMAS HEARNS, BOB & SUGAR RAY LEONARD

Well I never did get to go as much as I wanted to, but before they left the room, I had them pose on each side of me for a photo and when I realized they had their fists lifted on each side of my face, I broke into a look of fear that would have been oh so real had I actually had to go into the ring with either fighter. They both broke down laughing at me afterwards. Like many other photos that one hangs to this day in my den and I have to chuckle a little myself.

A few years later and now working in Detroit, I was in a local toy store trying to get some ideas for my boys' upcoming Christmas when who should I see coming my way down one of the aisles but Tommy Hearns. The guy had a cart simply overflowing with all measure of toys and games and I couldn't help but be taken aback a little. I mean here was this multimillion dollar boxing champ moving nonchalantly thru a suburban toy store with no fanfare or hype, just trying to be a good dad.

And still years after that while working for EMPIRE, I would regularly cover our local heavyweight contender "Baby" Joe Mesi. For a short time,

Leonard's promotional company was in charge of Mesi's career and we connected for several more interviews including a "live" half hour on the set of our daily "FAN-TV" afternoon program.

SUGAR RAY, BOB & BABY JOE MESI

Remembering that photo from 1989, I showed it to Leonard and he said let's do it again, this time with "Baby" Joe. Funny I sure seemed to have aged, but Ray looked even better than he did when I first met him 8 years earlier.

Hearns and Leonard were two of the professional fight game's most successful and prominent fighters, but to me they came across just like every day down to earth guys. And each had a story to tell with their words and their fists and did it masterfully.

TOM IZZO

CERTAIN individuals bring a smile to my face even at the mere mention of their name and one of those individuals is Michigan State's engaging Head Basketball Coach Tom Izzo.

Tom is a Northern Michigan native who you may or may not know grew up with another coach of note by the name of Steve Mariucci, the former Head Coach of the NFL's San Francisco 49ers. Like former Major League Baseball skipper Jim Leyland and former NFL Head Coach Jerry Glanville who were childhood friends in Perrysburg, Ohio, Tom and Steve have maintained their friendship throughout the years and have leaned on each other countless times for advice in a profession that is exceptionally stressful.

I first met Tom as an assistant to the equally legendary Jud Heathcote in East Lansing in 1983. At that time the Spartans played at storied old Jenison Field House in the years leading up to their move to their current home, the Jack Breslin Student Events Center. But before meeting Tom it was a tentative and nerve wracking introduction to Jud as he was putting his players through their paces during a midweek practice session.

It had been four years since Heathcote and Magic Johnson had brought the NCAA National Championship to MSU and Jud was as ornery as ever. As I entered the field house and stood with my cameraman underneath the running track above us, Jud noticed us and approached asking, "Who are you and what do you want?" I meekly answered, "Hi coach, my name is Bob Trimble and I'm the new Sports Reporter for WILX-TV working with Tim Staudt, our Sports Director". "Oh, ok fine, just stand over there and come over in a few minutes".

Now remember this was my first paying full time job in broadcasting and I was still literally learning the ropes and Tim had warned me in advance that Jud takes a little time to warm up to. But once he does and trusts you, you'll be fine. And that's when I spied Coach Izzo off to one side and approached him to introduce myself.

What a one-eighty that was from Jud. Tom, himself in his first season in the position, was as polite and gracious as his mentor was gruff and standoffish. I immediately felt a connection with Tom and that feeling remained for my time in Michigan for a trio of television stations as he eventually replaced Jud and began a career as a head coach at the university that is just incredible.

In his first eighteen years after taking over for Heathcote, Tom's success has been nothing short of amazing in terms of consistency. In 2000 his Spartans matched Jud's with a National Championship, returned to the title game in 2009 and had a total of seven Final Four appearances and equally as many Big Ten titles. And it was during that 2000 season championship tournament after my departure from WILX in Lansing and now working in Western New York at EMPIRE, that I experienced one of the highlights of my conversations with Coach Izzo.

It was game day at Detroit's Palace of Auburn Hills and thanks to the efforts of MSU Sports Information Director John Lewandowski, I was able to sit down with Tom for approximately twenty minutes at the team hotel. To my knowledge I was the only reporter to snare a "one on one" with coach on that game day and John pointed out that Tom liked me and my work and was more than happy to agree to that interview.

Now I am not saying it is in the best interest of either party (the interview or interviewee) to be the best of friends. But, a mutual respect as I have mentioned earlier, is a key to being able to co-exist. It allows when the time is right, to be able to get the interview that will separate you from other reporters and stations vying for the same insights.

I am proud that during my career that for the most part I had the ear of just about anyone I regularly covered and was able to "get" the information needed on a particular story whenever I needed it. There was a trust on both sides that played out with me gaining an edge over others attempting to do the same thing.

In the case of Tom Izzo, I have found no more of a cooperative sports personality and was always pleased to know that his respect for me was returned in kind.

EARVIN "MAGIC" JOHNSON

MAGIC. It describes Earvin Johnson perfectly. That now famous nickname was given to the NBA Hall of Famer by Michigan sportswriter Fred Stabley, Jr. and could not be more on target. Penned while Johnson was a brilliant high school prospect at Lansing's Everett High, it was given for the flair the kid brought to the game. His unique ball handling skills for a youngster who was much taller than others trying to guard him set him apart much like Wayne Gretzky's skating did in his formative hockey years.

Those considerable skills led him the short distance up the road to Michigan State and then of course during his thirteen year run as the leader of "Showtime" with the Los Angeles Lakers.

The gifted Johnson entered the NBA in 1979 after turning pro following his sophomore season with the Spartans, one in which he led them to the National Championship over Indiana State and another pretty darn good player by the name of Larry Bird. I had graduated from Ohio U. that same year and when I moved to Michigan got my first taste of what Magic there was in in this skinny, but oh so very talented favorite son.

While covering MSU athletics for Lansing's WILX-TV, I originally spoke to Johnson's former head coach, Jud Heathcote, about what he saw in Earvin that separated him from other college greats. He filled me in on what he felt made Magic such a special athlete and competitor as far as he was concerned and always did so with a sly smile. I mean, how fortuitous was it that this once in a generation talent would grow up in Michigan State's backyard?

BOB & MAGIC JOHNSON

Then each and every off season Johnson himself would return to his roots to host a basketball camp in his name for kids with buddies like former State teammate Scott Skiles. There we annually would take time out for an interview on not only the camp and the kids he loved so much, but mostly on the just completed NBA season.

Now remember, these were no ordinary off seasons for #32. He and the Lakers would go on to capture five NBA Championships in the 1980's and he was a perennial All-Star. More importantly from a league stand-point, he was one of the "faces" of the game's resurgence along with Bird of the Celtics and some kid named Jordan in Chicago. Recognized world-wide with that famous smile and easy going personality, he became and still is front and center in a variety of endeavors. Our conversations were very informative from what made him a dynamic performer on the court as well as away from it as a highly successful businessman.

I speak often about the word passion and how it pertains to those in this world that are leaders in their respective fields and it is the one constant that I find in each of them. Magic is the embodiment of that strength. Successful people often talk about their individual struggles along the path towards their goal and certainly nobody I have ever met has had more of a personal struggle than this man.

Right in the midst of his flamboyant and seemingly charmed professional basketball career, Magic was almost literally struck dead in his tracks in November of 1991 when he shocked the world with his announcement that he was HIV positive. It was a devastating revelation to those of us who knew the man and my own first thoughts went straight to "My God, is he going to die?"

Well we all know the answer to that question. A quarter century later Johnson is strong as ever having taken the necessary steps including medication to remain active and continuing to give back to his community. Among his business success stories is his part ownership of Major League Baseball's Los Angeles Dodgers.

Don't let that broad smile and boundless enthusiasm fool you as it did to countless opponents on the hardwood over the years and now in that business world. Earvin "Magic" Johnson is himself a killer when it comes to competition and what he wants to accomplish. He plays by the rules, but will also do whatever it takes to either make that shot, get that building built or contract signed. His life is a testament to that perseverance.

MICHAEL JORDAN

FROM the moment I saw Michael Jordan for the first time as a freshman in the 1982 National Championship game of college basketball for the University of North Carolina I admit I was totally mesmerized.

Basketball of the core four team sports in this country is fourth on my list to play or watch, yet seeing Jordan's ability even at that young age was a glimpse into the future. It was the future of a man who would arguably become the greatest player not only of his generation, but of all-time.

While working for television stations in Michigan in the 80's and 90's I had a front row seat to many contests featuring MJ as the unquestioned leader of one of the game's best teams ever, the Chicago Bulls. The statistics are staggering during that time span. Six NBA titles, a then record seventy-two victory season in 1995-96 & highlight reels that will be talked about a hundred years from now.

And while I personally believe that the simultaneous arrivals of Larry Bird & Magic Johnson in 1979 "saved" the NBA, it was Michal Jordan who took the baton and ran with it helping the league become global in appeal as well as marketability. I mean let's face it, would NIKE be where it is financially worldwide in the athletic shoe/sportswear business if not for "Air Jordan"?

So it was that at the Detroit Pistons' home of the Palace of Auburn Hills I would have the chance to interview Jordan time and again after his visits win or lose. However, unlike most of my interview subjects where I was able to gain one on one access, my conversations with Jordan were always part of a group of broadcasters. Radio and television reporters and camerapersons as well as newspaper writers were escorted into the cramped visitor's dressing room after the game was over.

I will be the first to admit I would have chosen to individually speak with him, but that opportunity would never present itself. Still, I was able to get my questions in and I can honestly say I have never met a more understanding and accommodating professional athlete.

Just picture a suspect cornered by the police with no escape route. That was what Michael Jordan had to endure eighty-two times a season not counting the playoffs. There were too many reporters with too many questions. You just had to be there to really grasp what this man had to endure, and I mean endure, on a nightly basis during the season.

Yet for all the inconvenience, the sauna like dressing room conditions which would make most of us melt inside our $2000+ designer suit and the relentless same questions over and over again, you could not find anyone more congenial to all of us in the assembled mass. He stayed until every last questions was asked and never complained. I know I couldn't have done it, probably would have cracked under such daily scrutiny. But give Michael credit, he never did once in my presence.

Long since retired (three different times) he is now the principal owner of the Charlotte Hornets and his philanthropic contributions are legendary as was his play on the court. I have the utmost respect for Michael Jordan and how he handled what for most of us would have been an impossible situation. A situation where because of his endless talent, his anonymity was taken away from him at an early age and never, ever will it return.

BRIAN KELLY

OF all the coaches I have met over the years, I have one that I can say I knew when he was just getting started as a graduate assistant in football at Grand Valley State University in Allendale, Michigan. His name is Brian Kelly who now calls South Bend home as the Head Coach at Notre Dame since 2009.

It was 1987 and I was in my third year in West Michigan at WZZM-TV and first as Sports Director. I had been covering the Lakers' program since 1985 and had developed a solid relationship with the current head coach, Tom Beck, who would eventually be elected to the College Football Hall of Fame.

Coach Beck would move to South Bend himself in 1991 for a single season as offensive coordinator under Lou Holtz. It was at that time he introduced me in the tunnel prior to the annual Notre Dame Spring Game to a freshman running back he thought was going to be a pretty good player for the Irish. His name was Jerome Bettis.

Tom would prove to be an excellent mentor to Brian who in just two years was promoted to defensive coordinator and recruiting coordinator. The thing that struck me about Brian from the start was his intelligence and attention to detail. He knew exactly what he wanted and developed programs to get his players on the same page almost immediately.

I always found Brian to be somewhat of a contradiction though. Away from the field you could not find a nicer guy with an easy going personality and smile. At several golf outings I participated in with he and Coach Beck to benefit the university, we laughed and joked all day while enjoying the gathering.

And he knew something about everything. He is as well rounded and learned an individual that I have ever known. From politics to football, do not get into a debate with Brian Kelly. He will shred you.

At the same time when focused specifically on football that was the key, focus. Brian is intense to a fault and single minded in his determination to have his team do things HIS way. And you cannot argue with success. Now I will not presume to say I knew one day he would become the head coach at one of the most storied programs in college football history, but I will say that hard work is what is necessary to become successful and nobody works harder than Brian Kelly at his job.

He would take over at Grand Valley as Beck's replacement when he left for Notre Dame and in thirteen seasons would win a pair of Division II National Championships including an amazing 41-2 record over his last three campaigns. Since that time it was on to continued success with both Central Michigan and then Cincinnati before the call came from the Irish and Brian was more than prepared to bring the Irish back to national prominence.

In 2010 long after my own career in broadcasting was in the rear view mirror, I had the opportunity to take my youngest son Jordan on a sixteenth birthday father/son trip that included a stop in South Bend. I had mentioned to a longtime coaching associate of Brian's, Mike Denbrock, who also was a friend from Grand Valley and later with the Arena Football league's Buffalo Destroyers, that I wanted to do something special for Jordan. Mike thought a trip to campus while he was playing high school football would be a great idea.

So arrangements were made with his help for a special day. Jordan and dad would tour Notre Dame Stadium including the locker room and the steps down to the field under the famous "Play Like a Champion" sign that all the players slap as they head outside. Jordan was very familiar with the setting as a fan of the popular movie "Rudy".

Stepping out on the field and looking around brought chills to both of us, especially me because of my lifelong following of the Irish program. It was like a dream. Look, there's Ara Parseghain on the home sideline shouting instructions to his defense. Look at the far end zone, "Rocket" Ismail just returned another kickoff for a touchdown . Oh Jordan, there's

Joe Montana, cool as ever leading another game winning drive. Yes just a dream, but it felt so real as we temporarily "woke up the echoes".

BOB, BRIAN KELLY & JORDAN

And then it was over to the incredible Guglielmino Athletic Complex where the coaches' offices are located. Inside "The Gug" I had the opportunity to introduce Jordan to Coach Kelly and it was a pretty special moment. Especially considering the fact that Brian was born in the Boston area and Jordan unknowingly had on his David Ortiz Red Sox jersey which brought a big smile to the coach's face. I had not seen Brian in person for several years, but was pleased there was instant recognition from him.

Since then the Irish have played for and lost the National Championship to Alabama, but the point is Notre Dame is back as a power in college football. And that is a testament to the work ethic and drive of the school's head coach Brian Kelly.

His staff continues to include Denbrock and Defensive Coordinator Brian Van Gorter, both of whom worked with Brian dating back to their days at Grand Valley State. So let's add loyalty to the list of the many strengths of Coach Kelly.

JIM KELLY

THE word toughness I feel is thrown around rather loosely in the sports world. Well let me tell you, to find real toughness look no further than the Hall of Fame quarterback of the Buffalo Bills, Jim Kelly.

The leader of the Bills famed K-Gun offense that earned four straight AFC Championships in the 1990's meaning four straight appearances in the Super Bowl, was tough as nails during his playing career and that carried over into his recent fight against cancer. While losing all four of those Super Bowls would have broken many, especially the anointed team leader, if anything I think it made Jim tougher than ever.

From afar I watched those Buffalo teams dominate like no other during the regular season with good friend and linebacker Ray Bentley of Grand Rapids taking part early on. However, he and his teammates would eventually be so very disappointed starting in Super Bowl XXV in Tampa not long after the beginning of the Gulf War in 1991. The Giants, Cowboys (twice) and Redskins sent the Bills down to defeat one after another.

These teams of fellow Hall of Fame coach Marv Levy were practically unstoppable from September to December. However, in January this rowdy bunch just appeared to implode in sometimes inexplicable fashion. How else do you explain as one example how running back Thurman Thomas's helmet simply vanished from the bench when he was preparing to go on the field at the start of Super Bowl XXVIII? It turned into a perfect storm of disaster come those Super Sunday's once Scott Norwood's field goal attempt to beat the Giants in Tampa sailed infamously "wide right" into the Florida night.

But through it all, General Jim Kelly persevered and led one of the most talented teams in history into that storm with help from fellow Hall of Famers like Levy, Thomas, Bruce Smith, Andre Reed, and most recently former General Manager Bill Polian.

Despite the mental and physical toll the game took on Jim, he never wavered in his determination to keep coming back like an old bulldog that gets smacked across the chops only to have at it once again. Yet Kelly's biggest challenge was away from the playing field in the person of his only son Hunter, who arrived on Valentine's Day, just like his daddy in 1997.

Hunter was born with a nervous system disease called "Krabbe Disease" which eventually took his life at the age of eight. Jim used his son's physical condition to start the Hunter's Hope Foundation which to date has raised awareness and millions of dollars for families all across the country dealing with this same and rare deadly disease. I personally took part in several Hunter's Hope events in Western New York and the love and support shown the Kelly family was to say the least, inspiring.

On several occasions Jim and his wife Jill joined me "on-set" at the EMPIRE studios in West Seneca to discuss Hunter's condition and what they hoped to accomplish on his and other children's behalf in the coming years. Obviously the fight in Hunter he got from his father as he did live to age eight when he wasn't originally expected to make it to his third birthday.

He also lived long enough to be on hand in Canton, Ohio in the summer of 2002 to see his proud papa inducted into the Pro Football Hall of Fame. In his acceptance speech Kelly famously said that "Hunter is my hero" in one of the most emotional speeches in the Hall's history.

The Kelly's welcomed me into their home as well as many appearances with me at EMPIRE. The annual Hunter's Hope Golf Event was always a special day with names including Montana, Marino and Jim's pal Chris (Nobody circles the wagons like the Buffalo Bills) Berman of ESPN among the annual participants.

Most recently Jim has come back yet again, this time from a form of oral cancer that sapped his strength, but not his will. It is a pleasure to say he is now cancer free after a two year struggle and as I said at the beginning, tougher than ever. "Kelly Tough".

For you kids and adults out there looking for a hero, a man standing up for himself, his family and what is good and right in the world, I direct you to Western PA native and now longtime Western NY resident, Jim Kelly.

MARIO LEMIEUX

WHILE Wayne Gretzky is considered the greatest hockey player ever, one of his rivals and peers during the 1980's and 90's sure had a lot to say about that recognition. Pittsburgh Penguins center Mario Lemieux was Gretzky's equal on many levels and in fact with his size and strength could have possibly eclipsed "The Great One's" overall numbers had his own health been better.

Lemieux who today is the principal owner of the Stanley Cup Champion Penguins' franchise battled back problems for most of his career with spinal disc issues and hodgkin's lymphoma, a cancer that caused one of his two premature retirements from the game.

And to put in perspective the games missed during just the regular season alone, Lemieux did not participate in some 513 contests. With his second best in NHL history of averaging just under a point per game that he did play, then you can see how "Le Magnifique" might well have fared when the numbers were all said and done over his 17 seasons in the league.

But we can't dwell on the negative because there are far too many positives for Mario from the time he debuted in 1984 to his final retirement in 2006.

Because of my duties in Detroit and Buffalo, I was able to witness first hand Lemieux's outstanding play in person in contests versus both the Red Wings and Sabres. And in my role as pre and post- game host specifically in Buffalo, I had the opportunity to sit down with Mario on several occasions to discuss his career. I found him to be a very quiet man who chose his words carefully never saying more than he intended to, but more direct and to the point than a lot of athletes who sometimes would talk your ear off in circles.

BOB & MARIO LEMIEUX

He was very candid about his play, his place in the game's great history and about his love of his second home of Pittsburgh and whatever it took to keep the Pens' franchise in the city for years to come.

My favorite Mario Lemieux moment, however, didn't come when I was working, but rather as a fan on New Year's Eve Day, December 31, 1988. At the now dismantled Mellon Arena or the "Igloo" if you prefer, the Penguins hosted New Jersey in an afternoon matinee battle. I had my oldest son Ryan with me and though he was just four years of age he does tell me today some things he remembers about that glorious afternoon.

You see Super Mario accomplished that day what no player before or since has. He scored five goals totaling eight points in every possible way you can score a goal. He tallied an even strength, power play, shorthanded, penalty shot and empty netter! It was truly amazing and considering I attended only three games that season, I certainly feel I got my money's worth.

You had to be in the building to feel the rush in the crowd every time

Lemieux touched the puck. The old Igloo was rocking from start to finish and of all the hockey games I ever attended, this was by far the best.

That's the memories I have of Mario, a superb athlete and fine man who played with incredible pain and discomfort throughout his career and still produced spectacular numbers and performances not to be forgotten.

Our Penguins are still here in Pittsburgh thanks to Lemieux's efforts both on and off the ice. He is the only man to win a Stanley Cup as a player and owner (twice each) and as one Steel City sportswriter penned it, Mario Lemieux is the "savior" of the Pittsburgh Penguins. And I for one say "Thank You Mario."

JOE NAMATH

AS the turbulent decade of the 1960's erupted into internal strife the likes of which this country had not seen since the Civil War, sports was certainly a welcome break for much of the population. And a brash and colorful professional football quarterback with shaggy hair & white shoes would be the primary figure besides Muhammad Ali to grab the attention of men and women alike.

His name was Joe Willie Namath of Beaver Falls, Pennsylvania, just across the river from where I was born in the neighboring community of New Brighton.

With the war in Vietnam raging out of control, protests by college students on campuses from Boston to Berkley and assassin's bullets gunning down a pair of American icons in civil rights leader Dr. Marin Luther King Jr as well as presidential candidate Robert Kennedy, I can clearly remember my mother and father talking many evenings about what was taking place after watching Walter Cronkite's report on CBS each weeknight.

It was at this time that I knew I wanted somehow, someway to be involved with the presentation of information like Mr. Cronkite. It was like a thunderbolt.

It was also around this time in the mid 60's that I began following sports on television & playing sports in what is known nationally now as a hotbed of athletic talent. Besides Joe, the names are a who's who list of notable stars from Western PA such as Mike Ditka, Pistol Pete Maravich, Norm Van Lier, Tito & Terry Francona, Tony Dorsett and some quarterbacks of note by the names of Blanda, Kelly, Marino, Montana & Unitas.

I was fascinated with Roberto Clemente of my hometown Pirates more than anybody, but he was a native of Puerto Rico. In "Broadway Joe" I had a guy to watch and read about from my own backyard as he dazzled opponents in the old American Football League.

In those years prior to the AFL-NFL merger it was much different than today with seemingly unending wall to wall sports coverage from networks to cable and of course the internet. You didn't just turn on the tube and get to see the Jets and Raiders for instance.

The AFL's television deal was primitive by today's standards so I relied more on the Sporting News for recaps and stats on how Joe was performing each week rather than seeing him "live" on our living room television screen. And to find out that mom had actually on a few occasions baby sat Joe when he was a youngster was just out of this world!

So when the opportunity finally at long last presented itself to meet and interview Joe in person long after his Hall of Fame playing career was over at a sports card & memorabilia show in suburban Detroit I made sure that my producers at WKBD-TV had a camera ready to go.

I had made arrangements through the show's promoter to meet with Joe upon his arrival for a few minutes before he would go out and meet his public. Prior to that, I contacted Joe's older brother Frank, who was at the time my mother's insurance agent. Frank would then get in touch with Joe at his home in Florida to advise of my request as well as indicate I was in fact from Beaver County and had a connection to the family.

It can be tricky sometimes using back channels to line up an interview, but at the same time there is a great deal of satisfaction and accomplishment when it all comes together as it did in this case.

JOE NAMATH & BOB

My cameraman & I were already in position when Joe walked in and introduced himself. Tanned and slender and not at all walking with any kind of noticeable limp from those horrific knee injuries and subsequent extensive surgical procedures, he still just oozed "cool" and once we sat down he asked how a Pittsburgh kid managed to be working in Detroit.

"Don't you want to be on-the-air back home instead of up here in Michigan?" I replied "Yes sir, just one problem." "What's that?" he shot back to which I replied it has been and always will be a goal of mine to be on the sports anchor desk in Pittsburgh at KDKA or WTAE or WPXI or the new KBL cable sports network now known as ROOT Sports .

But despite my best efforts the timing just hasn't been right for the folks on that end. Either a local talent actually living in the area would be hired or as was the case many times over for me, a minority or female was what the station or more likely station management was looking for.

Joe knew what I meant as he had been in front of the camera on his own New York talk show during his playing days as well as many other television and movie appearances over the years. "Keep trying Bobby. Don't give up if that is your dream." Namath did appear sincere in his hopes for me, and that just added to the good vibe I was getting from him and our interview went on very comfortably on both sides.

It was a treat hearing firsthand about playing for "Bear" Bryant at the University of Alabama followed by the first of several major knee injuries and arduous rehab along with a loss of mobility that would affect him in college and the pros. We discussed his debut in the bright lights of the "Big Apple" where his $427, 000 rookie contract was the largest ever at the time.

Then on to Super Bowl III and his famous "guarantee" the Jets would upset the highly favored Colts. The fact is it was an offhanded remark that picked up a life of its own & when it got back to Head Coach Weeb Ewbank, he was not a happy man. Of course we all know how that ended. The greatest upset in NFL history as the Jets shocked the Baltimore Colts.

Neither was Joe nine years later with an unceremonious end to his career with a forgettable final season in 1977 with the Los Angeles Rams. All in all a very revealing twenty minutes that actually ended up closer to thirty.

The only subject he would not address at all except to lower and shake his head and offer, "I have nothing to say about that", was my question on the recent acquittal of O.J. Simpson in the murder case of his ex-wife Nicole and her friend Ron Goldman. "Broadway Joe" and the "Juice" were once competitors against each other on the field and later partners in the broadcast booth on ABC's Monday Night Football and in fact enshrined in the Pro Football Hall of Fame on the same day in 1985.

But it was clear not to pursue the point any further. There was obvious pain in Joe's eyes and voice when the subject was brought up, so then and there I knew to simply back off and politely end our interview.

There are very few sports, entertainment or political figures I have met in my life that had that special aura about them that you could palpably feel being in their presence. Muhammad Ali and Joe Namath were those two for me. And just like Ali, I left this interview feeling pretty good about myself. I asked what I wanted to ask, got informative and sometimes surprising candor and felt as though my subject respected me as a journalist.

ARNOLD PALMER

ALSO hailing from the state of Pennsylvania, Latrobe specifically, is one of professional golf's greatest players and ambassadors, Arnold Palmer. The first real sports star of the emerging television age of the 1950's, Palmer brought the game into people's living rooms with a flair and enthusiasm not really seen in the sport previously.

Unlike team sports such as baseball or football, golf is an individual sport that was perceived by much of the population to be more for the wealthy and privileged as opposed to the working class. Arnie's arrival on the PGA Tour changed that way of thinking almost overnight. His popularity grew as the son of a greenskeeper who used to follow his dad around helping maintain the pristine Latrobe Country Club, to a fan favorite that developed one of the first ever fan clubs, "Arnie's Army".

Members in the gallery flocked to see their hero play, following closely from hole to hole and then erupting when he would hit a near perfect pitch shot or line up and drain a long putt. And while not quite as loud and rambunctious as those who jammed the tee box or green for Adam Sandler's movie character "Happy Gilmore", the Army helped promote Palmer's career just as much as the many lucrative endorsements he signed.

Having watched in awe on my television screen as Palmer and his long-time nemesis Jack Nicklaus dominated the tour in the 1960's and 70's, it was a treat to at last meet Arnie in person for the first time as the host of WZZM-TV's coverage of the inaugural Greater Grand Rapids Open. This was a Senior Tour event that began at the Elks Country Club in that Michigan community in 1986.

BOB & ARNOLD PALMER

Fifty-six years of age when I met him, Palmer was still twenty years from retiring from tournament golf and also very much a crowd pleaser. WZZM earned the television rights to the tournament, so it was a given that as host I would be afforded significant access to the golfers throughout the week. I conducted "live" post round interviews with the participants including some of the game's longtime stars including Gary Player, Chi Chi Rodriguez, Billy Casper, Sam Snead, & the eventual champion, the dapper and gentlemanly Jim Ferree.

But it was Arnold Palmer who I and the vast majority of fans came to see and he did not disappoint. The Senior Tour was designed for players fifty and older to compete for prize money that many times exceeded what was up for grabs during their days on the regular tour. Additionally, and no less important to the sponsors, was the opportunity to get up close and personal with these legends who were just happy to be able to continue making a living at the sport they treasured.

The first of many "sit down" interviews that week was with Arnie. In these settings you as a journalist have sole access at the time to your subject and the production staff at WZZM-TV was outstanding in their pre-interview set up. Providing everything from comfortable chairs positioned in the shade and out of the direct sun, to utilizing some of the best equipment in the business. They gave the "live" telecast and all surrounding "taped" features such as my one-on-one interviews a very polished and professional look. In fact that was one of the first things Palmer mentioned to me just before the cameras were rolling.

He noticed the preparation of our people and during the Pro-Am round earlier in the week as to tower placement of cameras and what seemed like miles of cable connecting every corner of the Elks beautiful layout. I am quite sure that professionalism impressed him and made for a wonderful interview. Very easy going and abundantly knowledgeable in all phases of game, I found speaking with him almost like a guided tour of PGA golf and its growth and impact.

His epic meetings with Nicklaus on the game's greatest courses worldwide were of great personal interest to me. And he was just astounding with his recollections of those matchups and locations and what the thought process was on particular shots. As a four time Masters champion and winner of ninety-five total tour events, that's a lot of information to process.

Without question there was a degree of animosity between the two men as Jack eventually passed Arnie's victory total. Like tennis, golf is so very much an individual sport, and rivalries develop and none was more competitive than those between these two. I discovered that as the years passed that the strain between Nicklaus and Palmer subsided to the point where they have developed a strong friendship that lasts to this day.

We would meet several more times in Grand Rapids over the next few years and when I eventually moved on to my time in Detroit at WKBD-TV, there were more conversations at the TPC of Dearborn and its annual Senior Tour stop.

Now in his 80's he has significantly slowed down, however, is just as popular to his legion of fans everywhere as he was in his playing heyday. Golf was originally labeled "a gentleman's game." If that is the case, then in my opinion, Arnold Palmer ranks as one the finest gentleman I have ever had the great fortune of meeting.

BARRY SANDERS

I unabashedly feel the greatest running back ever in professional football was Gale Sayers. No he did not have anywhere near the yardage of any of the top 25 rushers of all-time, nor have the power of Jim Brown or the longevity of Brown and any other current hall of fame running back. But in those brief 68 games before he finally had to step away because of multiple knee injuries, Gale was pure poetry and a joy to watch in the open field.

That said, I never saw Sayers in person on the field. I have old film clips and that is more than enough for me to base my opinion. However, if you want to talk about the greatest running back I ever actually did see in person in his prime and his entire career from start to finish, then hands down that's Barry Sanders.

From the time he burst onto the scene in 1989 as a Heisman Trophy winner out of Oklahoma State, Barry's ability to jab and juke and make defenders miss and grab at thin air, it was immediately clear to anyone who saw him play that this was a very special and gifted young man.

5 feet 8 inches and a rock solid 203 pounds, Sanders was low to the ground to begin with and once he took a handoff or swing pass out of the backfield you really never knew what was going to happen. He may have led all NFL running backs in yards lost in a career, but for every lost yard he made up for it with an explosive and elusive display that was nothing short of superhuman. Especially considering his #20 jersey was the primary target of the defenses of each and every Detroit Lions' opponent.

I came to Detroit as a Sports Anchor/Reporter in the fall of 1991 where Barry was already the club's star attraction. I had covered the Lions while in my previous career stops in Toledo, Ohio as well as Lansing & Grand Rapids, Michigan, but now would be doing so on a regular week in week out basis and was anxious to do so.

My first game in that role was on the afternoon of Sunday, November 17th inside the Pontiac Silverdome. The game was a 21-10 Lions' victory over the visiting Los Angeles Rams as Barry was anything but spectacular. He ran twenty- six times for a mere fifty-seven yards, his second lowest output of what would turn into the team's best season record of 12 and 3 and its' first playoff appearance since the year I came into this world in 1957!

What was memorable from that game was the devastating neck injury suffered by Detroit offensive lineman Mike Utley who famously flashed his "Thumbs Up" sign while being wheeled off the field. While still with us as a friend, inspiration and motivational speaker, Mike has never walked again.

Barry went on to become the league's third all-time leading rusher before his abrupt and shocking retirement behind Emmitt Smith & Walter Payton. And all the while I was there for the home games and many of the away games as well as practices and training camps (which Barry on more than a few occasions found a way to skip). We spoke in countless one on one situations after games and practices as well as pre-approved other more lengthy conversations.

Yet while I was always able to get him to comment on his game performances and that of the team, for the most part Barry was more of an introvert. Guys like one of his contemporaries, Deion Sanders (who by the way was being considered to draft instead of Barry in '89) to today's Richard Sherman of the Seahawks, never seemed to miss a chance to get on camera or in front of a microphone. But that wasn't Barry.

Just like Sayers (also very introverted during his playing career) Sanders was not into all the pomp and circumstance of being a nationally recognized bona fide star. Polite and quiet almost to a fault, just like Gale after one of his spectacular runs into the end zone he followed (always) with a simple flip of the football to the official before trotting to the sidelines.

After bidding adieu to the Motor City in 1998 headed to Western New York I still followed the Lions' and specifically Barry and again like most, was just floored when on the doorstep of breaking the all-time rushing record held at the time by Payton he called it quits. So after ten amazing seasons that included joining the rarified 2000 yard club in 1997, he simply walked away from the game while very much able to continue playing.

It is a very personal decision to retire from one's profession and I would never presume to tell Barry or anyone else for that matter when to do it. But the way in which the announcement was made, through his hometown Kansas newspaper in the form of a fax was unprofessional to me. Once he knew he wasn't coming back I believe he owed it to his coaches and teammates to advise, especially with the NFL Draft coming up in April of 1999.

Instead Sanders waited to send that fax to the paper until the end of July as the team was well into training camp for the upcoming season. No matter what the reason, which turned out to be his displeasure with the "losing culture" perception within the organization, how the whole scenario shook out was just wrong.

Nonetheless, Barry is now back in the good graces of the team and the city where he and his family still reside. And putting the retirement fiasco to the side, I will always have a big smile on my face watching and re-watching tape of Barry ever so nimbly navigating through enemy territory off on one of his signature jaunts to pay dirt. Thanks for those memories #20.

MIKE SCHMIDT

WITH apologies to fellow Hall of Famer Brooks Robinson, in my opinion the finest all around third baseman in Major League Baseball history was Mike Schmidt. Unquestionably the longtime Orioles' great had a consistent flair all his own defensively. Yet it is Michael Jack Schmidt who demonstrated his own brand of outstanding defensive play combined with unparalleled power at the plate. Power that saw him slam 548 career home runs until his retirement in 1989. No steroids here, just good old fashion work & some pretty amazing god given talent.

I first met Mike on the afternoon of September 30, 1978 at Pittsburgh's Three Rivers Stadium when the visiting Philadelphia Phillies were in town to take on my hometown Pirates. This was the fourth game of a five game series on the next to the last day of the season with the National League East Pennant at stake. A win and the hated cross state rival Phillies would win their third consecutive title. And that's exactly what happened, a 10 to 8 slugfest in favor of the visitors leaving a meaningless regular season finale the following day.

But my own spirits were much brighter in the hours prior to the first pitch as by now I had developed a great relationship with the Pirates Media Relations Department and was back to get more interviews and insights for my show on Ohio University's All Campus Radio Network. And who better to talk to than Bobcats' alum Mr. Schmidt who exited the Athens campus three years before my arrival as a freshman in 1975.

And Mike was all I had hoped he would be, cordial as well as focused on exactly what I was asking. From growing up in Dayton to the development of his baseball skills, we chatted about Ohio U's influence on him as opposed to skipping college, to a brief stay in the minors and then on to Philadelphia.

BOB & MIKE SCHMIDT at Spring Training in Clearwater, FL

At the time I wasn't sure how to take a tip he gave me as we were wrapping up our conversation around the batting cage. But looking back, his "fatherly advice" now seems poetic. Schmidt offered that being a junior in college in broadcasting might not necessarily be my actual road taken out into the real world. He suggested that forces or situations entirely out of my control could steer me to another career path. However, if I had singular focus and tireless preparation such as he invested in his chosen path to play professional baseball, I had every bit as much of a chance to succeed. Also toss in a little luck and timing for good measure.

Well, it turns out he was prophetic indeed. A call from the Head Coach and General Manager of the IHL's Kalamazoo Wings, Bob Lemieux, during the latter half of my senior year got the ball rolling. I would accept a position as Ice Events Coordinator at Kalamazoo's home rink of Wings' Stadium. Knowing of my broadcasting dreams, Bob also hooked me up with the GM of the town's beautiful music radio station WQLR where I would get a shot at overnight weekend shifts as a DJ.

I then landed a color commentator spot for local high school football at a Battle Creek station for twenty-five dollars a game during the fall and at that point my days (and nights) were full. Thank you Mike for helping a young buck to believe in himself and put forth the effort to get started in the career I always aspired to as a youngster.

Mike Schmidt went on to win a World Series, participate in a dozen all-star games and win league Most Valuable Player honors three times. He even smacked his 500th career homer at Three Rivers in 1987 and then capped off his career with enshrinement in Cooperstown in 1995. Certainly a long way from that September afternoon in 1978 and I was glad to have had the chance to meet Mike in the midst of building that impressive resume.

ALAN TRAMMELL

IN the magical year of 1984, The Detroit Tigers won the World Series and I began my broadcasting career with my first full time position as the Weekend Sports Anchor/Weekday Sports Reporter for Lansing, Michigan's WILX-TV. And it was at this time that I first met the man who would eventually become the MVP of that World Series, shortstop Alan Trammell.

"Tram" as he was known to teammates and fans was the model for what a professional athlete should be. I have met all types over the years and other than "Mr. Hockey" Gordie Howe, I have ALWAYS said that he and Alan Trammell are absolutely the best professional athletes that I have ever known.

Not the biggest, the strongest, the fastest and certainly not the most intimidating presence, Tram made the most of his abilities and produced a twenty year career that statistically speaking was one of the best ever by a major league shortstop. In fact, The New Bill James Historical Baseball Abstract has ranked him the ninth best shortstop of all-time which puts him ahead of fourteen other shortstops who are already members of the Hall of Fame.

When I think of Trammell I think of consistency, which is the hallmark of what every athlete I think wants to be remembered for. Along with second baseman Lou Whitaker, that duo played more games (1,918) and more seasons (19) together than any double play combo in the long history of the game.

They were the cornerstone defensively of one of the greatest teams ever. A "team" that manager Sparky Anderson assembled with every last player playing an important role in Detroit's overall success. The 1984 Tigers won more games than any previously in the franchise with 104 and that World Series crown was the first in the Motor City since 1968.

Names like Kirk Gibson, Jack Morris, Lance Parrish, Chet Lemon as well as Cy Young and MVP winner Willie Hernandez led the charge along with Trammell and Whitaker. An incredible 35 and 5 start that may never be approached again, a Morris no-hitter at old Comiskey Park on the first Saturday of the season and Detroit was off and running.

ALAN TRAMMELL & BOB at Spring Training in Lakeland, FL

I sat down with Tram on many occasions with more in-depth inter-views of course during Spring Training in Lakeland, Florida. There at Joker Marchant Stadium with the palm trees blowing in the soft breeze in the outfield it was as perfect a setting as you could ever imagine. One particular interview session stands out above the rest because as Alan and I were talking, he paused and advised me to turn around and there I saw the trail of the launch of the Space Shuttle Discovery from the Kennedy Space Center against a beautiful cloudless sky.

Why do I remember it so well? It was my thirty second birthday, March 13, 1989. And because moments after Trammell told me to turn around, it seemed as though the entire roster came racing out of the dressing rooms adjacent to right field to see in person what they were witnessing on the television coverage inside. It made for a unique interview for the WZZM-TV broadcast that evening.

Whether it was in Florida or Detroit or Minneapolis or Cleveland or whatever the venue, if I was covering the Tigers there was a good chance that part of the story would be Alan Trammell. A leader on and off the field, his Hall of Fame worthiness might be a question mark, yet it is a player exactly like him that I would want on my team. Never involved in controversy and always looking for what was best for his team, not personal statistics or notoriety, he was a major factor in the Tigers' success for the better part of two decades.

Beloved Detroit television News Anchor, the late Al Ackerman, coined a phrase that championship season of "Bless You Boys". I feel it was a blessing to have interacted with Alan Trammell who helped give me an up close and inside look at Major League Baseball and in particular a 1984 season that brought that city together like never before.

DICK VITALE

IN all my sports travels I certainly made my share of mistakes or incorrect assessments and none more than my first impression of college basketball broadcast legend, Dick Vitale. Before actually meeting the man in person, I thought the guy was just too much, talked too much, too much over the top, the broadcast is all about me.

The creator of such memorable lexicons such as "PTP'ER" & "Awesome Baby", Dickie V moved from college and professional basketball coaching into broadcasting as ESPN was in its' infancy in 1979 and has never looked back. Credit the network for many innovations over the years and the production of on-air talent that is some of the best ever. But also give credit to Vitale, who once given the opportunity behind the mic, turned the games he telecast into "events" that sometimes took on a life of their own.

During my coverage of the University of Michigan's "Fab Five" I had several interview opportunities with Vitale. One of the most memorable was in Minneapolis for the 1991 NCAA Final Four. In the media hotel I was coming down an escalator when who should I hear in conversation but that man Vitale in a coffee shop type setting in the lobby. He was surrounded by primarily local and national writers as opposed to broadcast types such as me.

My cameraman Mike Wood and I were simply heading to grab some breakfast before departing for the Metrodome to cover team practice when we realized what a great informal opportunity to get some thoughts from college basketball's unofficial spokesman. So as Mike hurried back up to our room to get his equipment, I cozied up to the group of writers and listened in taking some notes for my own soon to be asked questions if Dick would agree to it.

The timing could not have been more perfect because just as the writers broke up and went their separate ways, I corralled Vitale and he said he was more than happy to stick around for a few more minutes. We set up our camera in the lobby by some comfortable couches and even a small waterfall. For the next fifteen to twenty minutes I don't think I asked more than four questions and just stared in amazement as he pontificated on everything from the "Fab Five's" baggy shorts and nationally recognized swagger to his own influence on the way the game was covered.

DICK VITALE & BOB

I was truly mesmerized and when our interview was done I sincerely thanked him for his time he asked if I had any children and if so wanted to drop a little something in the mail once he returned home after the tournament was over. I readily admitted I didn't know what to say and simply offered a, "Mr. Vitale you don't have to do anything like that, I just appreciated you taking a few minutes to give us some of your insights into what we should expect". He just brushed off my reaction and said write down their names and ages and our address in suburban Detroit. So I did and really didn't think anything of it.

A few weeks later after the basketball season was over and I had moved on to covering the Tigers' baseball season I came home from work one day to find a big package on our front porch that my wife and kids were unaware had been dropped off. When I brought it inside the boys came running to greet me and when I said their names were all on the box they tore into that thing like it was Christmas morning. Inside were 3 Dick Vitale licensed regulation size basketballs. There was one each for Ryan, Brandon & Jordan.

There was also a copy of that season's college basketball season preview of ESPN the magazine autographed by Dick to me. Taken aback, you bet I was and while I certainly sent off a letter thanking Dick for the generous and unexpected gift, I also had each of my sons write up a little "thank you". What a treat for them and boy did those basketballs get used on our driveway until they simply wore out.

A year later it was back at the "Final Four", this time in party town New Orleans where it should be illegal to have so much fun. Sure there was the work to cover another Michigan appearance by Chris Webber and company, but there was also the city to visit including world famous Bourbon Street and Jackson Square.

On the Sunday between the National Semi Finals and the Championship Game, my crew and I had time to enjoy the nightlife "The Big Easy" was so well known for. We saw revelers of all kind including media members such as myself from the local and national scene as well as figures from the sports world and of course the hoard of fans from each of the represented schools from Ann Arbor to Chapel Hill.

Walking down the middle of the street with his arms around a pair of fans was former NFL quarterback Jim Plunkett who was the MVP of Super Bowl 15 just down the street at the Superdome when his Raiders had disposed of the Eagles many years earlier. And on a restaurant patio there was UNLV's controversial head coach Jerry Tarkanian engulfed by autograph and photo seeking fans.

As I turned to the opposite side of Bourbon Street on another restaurant patio there sat Dickie V surrounded as well by his adoring public. Now we would sit down the very next day for another pre-championship game interview as the Wolverines were set to try and win their first title after falling short as freshmen the year before to Duke. This time the opponent would be North Carolina.

But first on this night, I was able to get up close enough to say hello and thank him for what he did for my boys a year earlier and as if he'd known me all his life he lept up and gave me a firm handshake and big hug equally thanking me for my kind words. I will never forget that night, ever.

Dick Vitale and I spoke several more times over the next few years and each time it was really like greeting an old friend. He is sincere in his approach and unless you have actually met him, you really don't fully understand that. I do now. He is and always will be the unofficial ambassador for college basketball.

STEVE YZERMAN &
THE RED WINGS

WHILE working in Detroit at WKBD-TV and WJR-Radio I was fortunate enough to be in the midst of some the greatest individuals and teams the city has ever produced. And none were more than the creators of the nationally recognized moniker of "Hockeytown", the Detroit Red Wings.

From the time I entered broadcasting as a professional in 1983 I was constantly peppered with the name of the leader of those Red Wings' teams, their longtime captain by the name of Steve Yzerman. From the time he took over the "C" on his jersey for the 1986-87 season until his retirement in 2006, "The Captain" was one of the most talented and dedicated athletes I have ever witnessed.

Consistency to me is the hallmark of a great athlete and no one in any team sport was more consistent than #19. The best example of that is the fact he was captain for Detroit for some 1300 games and that is the most by any individual in a team sport in professional sports history in North America. He was a Hall of Famer in my eyes from the time he stepped on the Joe Louis Arena ice and officially became a member of Hockey's Hall of Fame in his first year of eligibility in 2009.

From his rookie season beginning in 1983 thru 1997 I had the great pleasure of watching Yzerman weave his magic like a tapestry, a true blueprint for success. During his career he found himself at times surrounded by some of the finest all around talent the game has ever produced from fellow forwards such as Sergei Fedorov, Brendan Shanahan, Chris Chelios, Brett Hull and Luc Robitalle. Add to that defensemen such as Paul Coffey and Nick Lidstrom and goalies including Mike Vernon and Chris Osgood and the winningest coach in NHL history, Scotty Bowman, and it was really a magical time in the Motor City.

I found Steve to be a quiet leader, a guy who showed his teammates what needed to be done on the ice as opposed to a vocal or verbally demonstrative personality. That's not to say when the hammer needed to be laid down he didn't or couldn't do it, but it really wasn't something that ever was regularly necessary. Yzerman was one of those leaders that truly led by his example as a player and gentleman.

To this day I challenge you to find any coach or player in the National Hockey League that has a negative word to say about Steve. That in and of itself should paint a pretty significant picture of a man that played the game at its highest level to the best of his god given ability. He did it with a class that few others in any team sport have ever shown.

I spoke with Steve on more occasions than I can count and he was nothing if not forthright and honest about his team's play or his own. He was readily critical if he felt he had not done enough to bring victory to Detroit, but in all honesty there were very few nights that the Red Wings didn't win in the 1990's. There was a rivalry in particular with the Colorado Avalanche that was as intense and deep seeded as any in professional sports annals.

Seeing in person what drove these two clubs at each other was the road to the Stanley Cup. At times it was beautiful, hockey as it should be played with speed and grace. And at others it was right out of the movie "Slapshot". A brutal case of will upon will. Who would falter just slightly enough for the opponent to take advantage of?

I watched from the press box as Claude Lemieux just buried a defenseless Kris Draper into the boards in Denver in the playoffs, his face no match for the immovable object that crushed bones under the force of its contact. A cheap shot if ever there was one that left the unaware Draper crumpled on the ice. I then observed months later on opening night in Detroit when Draper's best friend on the team, Darren McCarty, lined up in the opening face-off outer circle and glared towards Lemieux prior to the puck drop.

He told me later he said to Claude, "You ready, because I'm going to kick your ass!" And at the moment the puck dropped McCarty with a rage that had built up over an entire off-season proceeded to pummel Lemieux into submission before having to be pulled off of his hated nemesis by most of the officiating crew. The Red Wings of that era had each other's back and then some.

Other items that stood out as lasting impressions were simple things that might not be noticed by the casual observer. Guys that did not actually win the cup, but were important cogs in the elevation of the team to what it became were names like Keith Primeau, Paul Coffey and Dino Ciccarelli.

Coffey, himself a future Hall of Fame defenseman and multiple Stanley Cup winner with Edmonton and Pittsburgh, would stay after practice and skate figure eights forward and backward on the ice so many times I got dizzy. He would work with youngsters such as Mike Sillinger in the techniques of playing defense. Again all this after practice had long been over.

Then there was Dino. Just think of that bulldog who sticks his nose into things knowing he is going to get the crap beat out of him while dishing out some punishment of his own. That was Dino Ciccarelli. I always felt bad he didn't get a ring because he was a workhorse in front of the opposition's net.

After practice he would take shot after shot from every conceivable angle from a teammate and attempt to redirect it past the goalie. He would then take that practice into games where he would get blasted from side to side, checked, stuck with a stick in the ribs or worse. He would still keep his wits about him to either redirect a shot in for a goal or perhaps cause enough chaos in front of the net that the opposing goaltender would never see a shot at all that eventually scored.

Just go back and watch video of his countless meetings with Blackhawks' goalie Eddie Belfour. Those two absolutely hated each other and on more than one occasion it was Dino who took the wrath of Belfour to his privates with a stick. And Dino never backed down.

These players along with role players such as Mike Knuble, Kirk Maltby and physical talents such as Joey Kocur and the late Bob Probert all in some way, shape or form combined to eventually build a three time Stanley Cup Championship team with victories in 1996, 97 and 2002. Again I go back to that word consistency. These Red Wings were beyond consistent. They simply took over the league for several seasons thanks in large part to Yzerman and his teammates.

A final thought on Steve that is of a more humorous nature. Now you will hear players and coaches alike say that they do not read the sports section of the local newspapers or watch the television sports segments or listen to the radio regarding how the team is doing. That is not entirely true. They do and one reason I know is that it almost got me killed while standing behind the Wings' bench during a practice at Joe Louis Arena.

As I was watching while trying to formulate a "stand-up" that I was going to do as a part of that evening's feature on the team I happened to look up in just enough time to see Steve fire a puck in my direction from across the ice. In an instant that puck whizzed by my right ear and caromed off the glass behind me. Yes, much like my experience while standing in goal against Gordie Howe in that "One on One" exhibition in Muskegon, I urinated myself.

Apparently Steve had watched a recent feature I did on "Ice Golf" being played on a local lake that had drawn the attention of hundreds of men from all over the area to take part in. I, thinking it appropriate because it was ice, it was cold and the lake was frozen, decided to wear a Jaromir Jagr jersey from my hometown Pittsburgh Penguins for the event.

Well the Captain took offense to my choice of wardrobe and made it clear with that puck stunt that if I was going to be wearing a hockey sweater in the future it would be that of a Detroit Red Wing. I never had an opportunity to do another story for my remaining days in Detroit that could possibly require me to wear a hockey jersey, but I got the message.

Steve made it perfectly clear that his heart and mine darn well better be filled with red and white if there was hockey or any variation of it to be played in the Motor City.

Again I was proud to have been there with Yzerman and his incredibly talented mates to raise that Stanley Cup and be a part of the celebrations that followed as the official television station that carried the games all season long. It was a very special time indeed to be a part of "Hockeytown".

THE ACTORS

JAMES CAAN & SHELLEY FABARES

BRIAN Piccolo and Sonny Corleone, could two men be any less similar? Piccolo, the tragic real life football figure of the acclaimed "Brian's Song" made for television movie in 1971. Corleone, the hot headed mafia son in 1972's Best Picture of the Year,"The Godfather".

The common thread was the actor who portrayed both brilliantly, James Caan.

A high profile member of the Hollywood scene for over fifty years, in person, much to my surprise he was very much down to earth and as pleasant as any celebrity I have ever spoken with. We met in East Lansing, Michigan in the fall of 1987 as Caan was back on campus to serve as Grand Marshall of the university's homecoming parade.

BOB & JAMES CAAN

While he attended, but did not actually graduate from MSU, he was nonetheless a noteworthy former student and I was able to sit down with him for a few minutes in the school's football offices. I found him to be very candid about his career and overall zest for life and challenges.

Of course my primary questions had to deal with his participation in "Brian's Song" and the impact it had in me at the time in the aftermath of my father's recent death. Again, he showed surprising compassion for me and really gave a great background into his role and what working alongside Billy Dee Williams was like. He credited a great screenplay by Bill Blinn as well as the personal influences of the real Gale Sayers and Brian's widow, Joy, during production.

Ironically several years later, I was able to meet actress Shelley Fabares who portrayed Joy Piccolo in the movie. Shelley was well established as an actress including a trio of movies with Elvis Presley and singer, who rose up the charts in 1962 with her hit recording of "Johnny Angel". James' very kind words for her at the time proved absolutely true.

BOB & SHELLY FABARES

In Detroit to host an Alzheimer's Disease benefit banquet, Shelley spoke poignantly about her own experience with the disease as it was the eventual cause of her mother's death. After her speech I introduced myself and mentioned my conversation years earlier with Caan about "Brian's Song" and she too could not be more complimentary of him. She was simply angelic herself, warm and sweet.

Looking back now I find it ironic that the film itself has had such a deep impact on me to this day relating to its timing and my dad's passing due to heart disease. At the same time, in the movie, Joy loses Brian to cancer while in real life Shelley, her mom to Alzheimer's.

If you take a look at the opening sequence in "Brian's Song", narrator Jack Warden (who portrayed Head Coach George Halas in the film) states, "Ernest Hemingway once said every true story ends in death. Well this is a true story." And it all really was.

BILL COSBY

It is important to note here that my encounters with comedian Bill Cosby occurred many years before the sexual misconduct charges were filed against him and made public. But at that time the way I and really the whole world viewed him and what he stood for were very much in a positive light.

Over the years I have seen him perform his trademark stand-up comedy at a variety of different venues. The first came while I was still a college student at the very intimate outdoor amphitheater on the Beaver campus of Penn State University just a few short miles from the home I grew up in. While actually in school at the time in Ohio, when my mother advised that Bill was coming to Beaver County I immediately said get me a ticket! First come first serve bench seating gave me the chance to get a front row seat and for over an hour and a half I was in heaven, eating up every joke and story.

Mind you, even though I am also a fan of Richard Pryor, George Carlin & Eddie Murphy, Cosby's shows have always been able to be seen by anyone at any age. There never was an expletive uttered and still, at every tour stop his shows were sellouts.

Fast forward to the late afternoon of April 9, 1989 as I am typing away my scripts for the upcoming 6 o'clock Eyewitness News sports segment for WZZM-TV when there is a knock at my door and in walks my News Director Jack Hogan. He says, "Bobby you will not need to anchor tonight's

11pm sports report." Well, always the worrier, I thought oh geez what's wrong, what did I do? Turns out I did nothing bad, I was actually being rewarded. I was informed that for Bill Cosby's "In the Round" concert at Muskegon's L.C. Walker Arena that evening, I was to represent the station (one of the Cosby show's sponsors) and go out on stage and introduce him to the audience and then stay and enjoy his show.

To say the least, I was astounded. Apparently station management found out how much I enjoyed Cosby and waited until the last moment to let me in on their plans. So I blew through the early newscast (I swear I don't remember even doing it) and it was off to Muskegon about a 20 minute drive right next to Lake Michigan.

BILL COSBY & BOB

Knowing I was coming, security led me to the dressing room door and there he was, Bill Cosby in a comfortable sweater from the Lake Placid 1980 Olympic Games. He got up from the couch and invited me in. It was just the two of us and I was a little nervous. I know he sensed it so he just asked me to tell me a little about myself and what I did. I know he knew

I was from the local television station, but other than that, nothing else. Once we started talking he basically laid it out for me. "Just go out there and say anything you want about me. I will follow your lead. The folks know me, now you know me. Just make it personal & I will follow your lead, ok? I said, "great, I can do that." It was most certainly an evening to remember.

Our next encounter came at the Palace of Auburn Hills just north of Detroit and the home of the Detroit Pistons. It was a game night and I was situated in my normal seat courtside with other media members to the left and behind the Pistons' bench. This is where I would take game notes and time codes coordinated with my WKBD-TV cameraman. Then after the game we could assemble our package using game footage I wanted specifically timed to the play and add interviews from the dressing room.

Also seated close by was my tape editor Tom O'Neal who was not working that evening, but a passionate sports fan of the Pistons and Lions and when he could get a "press pass" to a game he would never miss a chance to go. In attendance that night was Cosby who was the guest of Pistons' owner, the late Bill Davidson. Mr. Davidson put on no airs whatsoever and fans loved that. He was very approachable, but with Cosby by his side there was some extra security to allow them to watch the game without being hassled by fans looking for an autograph or photo.

At halftime we usually would head to the media lounge for some refreshments, and just as we got up Cosby and Davidson approached. Bill then made Tommy's night as he broke into the voice of his cartoon character Fat Albert and said, "Hey, hey, hey." looking directly into Tom's eyes.

Tom, by the way, let's just say was and is a big man and when he let out a huge laugh, Cosby smiled right back at him, knowing no disrespect was meant and moved on.

That's the Bill Cosby I choose to remember. The man that could make you laugh about normal everyday things in your life that you might not give a second thought to. Sadly, in today's landscape, others will only remember him for his rapid fall from grace. A fall amidst allegations that fly directly in the face of the persona he perpetuated during a more than half century in the entertainment industry.

JAMIE FARR

Much like Arthur Fonzarelli ("The Fonz") from the television series "Happy Days", Corporal Max Klinger of "M-A-S-H" television fame was originally not supposed to appear in more than just a few episodes. However, thanks to their originality and the cries of fans everywhere, both went on to become staples of those respective iconic series.

Klinger, the cross dressing mad man of the 4077 was played by Jamie Farr, the favorite son of Toledo, Ohio. And while he became as much of a household name as sidekicks Hawkeye, Trapper, B.J., Hot Lips and Radar, those Toledo roots that he so often mentioned on the series were not an act at all.

JAMIE FARR & BOB

I was in my first and only year of work at WDHO-TV (now WNWO), the ABC affiliate in Toledo when Farr and the Ladies Professional Golf Association (LPGA) teamed up for the inaugural Jamie Farr Toledo Classic. The tournament featured some of the biggest names in the game at the time such as Nancy Lopez, Jan Stevenson, Amy Alcott and Beth Daniel.

And Jamie was much more than a name plastered on a billboard advertising the event early that July at Glengarry Country Club. He was very much an active participant promoting the event and its primary charity, The Ronald McDonald House of Northwest Ohio.

When I interviewed him several times before, during and after that first event, the enthusiasm and sincerity about his pride for his hometown and the people was at the forefront. He without question appreciated all the attention that his acting career and in particular Corporal Klinger brought to the city and while the name and sponsors may have evolved over the years, children's charities in Ohio and Michigan have benefitted to the tune of six million dollars plus since the tournament began.

GILL HILL

I first saw Gill Hill on-screen as Inspector Todd in the highly successful and entertaining motion picture "Beverly Hills Cop" while living in Toledo in 1984. I remember it vividly because I watched it with my friend Kurt Kleinendorst, a member of the Toledo Goaldiggers, the city's minor league professional hockey team, who went on to a very successful career as an assistant and then head coach for a number of franchises.

Hill meantime was not a fulltime actor. He actually was a Detroit police detective at the time and I cannot picture anyone else filling the roll of Todd like Gill did in all three of the Eddie Murphy starring movies. Though to be honest, I think even Gill would agree that while Cop I and Cop II were pretty good action and comedic entertainment, the third installment was just death which is appropriate since Inspector Todd indeed dies in that film.

I moved on from Toledo to Grand Rapids and eventually Detroit where I became friends with Gill after meeting him at Opening Day festivities for the Tigers at Tiger Stadium in the early 1990's. By that time he had traded in his badge for a political career that saw him elected to the Detroit City Council in 1989 where he eventually was elected President. He also ran for Mayor of Detroit in 2001, but was unsuccessful in that bid.

GILL HILL & BOB

Gill was gracious enough to join me one time on my "Sports Xtra" show on WKBD-TV to talk about the Detroit sports scene, but also my own interest in the "Beverly Hills Cop" franchise. Now if you have seen any of those movies you know that Inspector Todd uses profanity like most of us use air to breathe. It is non-stop, but I never found it offensive as that is just the way it is, actually much more true to life than what you might get on network television "censored" offerings. The funny thing is Gill was quick to point out that he never wanted his grandchildren to see him in that character primarily due to his foul mouth. That would burst the bubble so to speak of the fatherly and protective person he was in their eyes.

PAUL NEWMAN

Among these most opportune encounters with motion picture and television personalities, came my visit with Paul Newman in the summer of

1989. The veteran actor, producer, philanthropist, and professional race car driver was in West Michigan for some testing at Belding's Grattan Raceway.

At the time Newman was working with Trans-Am Series car owner Bob Sharp and driving alongside Sharp's son Scott who would go on to his own success in the coming years in a variety of styles of racing.

Previously I also had the pleasure of catching up with another race enthusiast at Grattan, who had a career also primarily in another field of endeavor. That was the great Hall of Fame running back of the Chicago Bears, the late Walter Payton.

But on this pleasant weekday afternoon my focus was on the star of some of my personal favorites films such as "Cool Hand Luke", "Butch Cassidy and the Sundance Kid" and "The Sting". Very slight of build on his 5 foot 10 inch frame he looked every bit the part of a race driver, save for his almost completely white head of hair.

Having been informed by the track owners of his unpublicized appearance, and knowing of Newman's disdain for the media in general, I must admit I was slightly apprehensive about making contact. And so not long after his arrival to test his and his car's abilities on the two mile curvy and hilly course, I approached Paul and introduced myself and asked if he had a few minutes to talk about his visit.

BOB & PAUL NEWMAN

To my surprise while he did still seem a bit guarded, Newman agreed under the condition that this interview or clips from it would be run only on WZZM-TV. It would not be sold or made available to the networks for national coverage. I had no issues at all with his request.

So for approximately twenty minutes he commented very candidly regarding his second career behind the wheel and the need for focus on the track every bit as much as delivering his lines in one of his incredible array of movie projects. He added that while racing provided a "release" it also was not a business to be taken lightly. He immersed himself into the sport and went on to co-own Newman-Haas Racing on the Indy Car Circuit for many years with partner Carl Haas.

I concluded the session by asking how difficult it was for him to separate work and his major celebrity status from being as much of a "regular" guy as possible away from the Hollywood scene. He again in his own quiet and reserved way explained that the so called "scene" was never an issue for he and his wife and fellow actor Joanne Woodward. They preferred to make their home on the east coast in Connecticut where they could read and write plays at their own pace. With their mutual success they could certainly afford to do so.

Paul Newman impressed me in person primarily because he was one of the few people I have ever met in my lifetime who truly seemed happy. A man with what appeared to be a perfect balance of work ethic and personal contentment. Yet he also was regularly looking for that next stimulating challenge.

Then, just like that, he gave me a firm handshake and was gone, only to re-appear minutes later in his red, white and blue fire retardant suit. And with helmet and gloves in hand he climbed into Bob Sharp's Trans-Am for what he actually came to West Michigan to do, that is only after taking a slight detour to satisfy my request.

TOM SELLECK

Another actor with Detroit ties who is still going strong into his seventh decade is the very popular Tom Selleck. Born in Detroit and like Jamie Farr's character Klinger, while playing private detective Thomas Magnum in the "Magnum P.I." series, Selleck was very seldom seen minus his Detroit Tigers' cap. In fact he even got Alan Trammell and Lou Whitaker cameos on one of the shows. And I am sure it was Whitaker who made sure they would be paid for that appearance. I will have more on him shortly.

It was that Tigers' connection that brought him to town in the early 1990's to appear at a sports memorabilia show at Cobo Hall with a later in the day visit to the stadium to take some batting practice with the team prior to a game.

I made arrangements to get a camera from WKBD to do a feature package on Tom's appearance and was hoping that the persona that he projected on screen was what the man was like off camera. He did not disappoint. I met a guy who had an exceptionally easygoing personality and a smile that appeared to be genuine, not forced.

TOM SELLECK & BOB

When he arrived I had already set up time to steal Tom away for a few minutes of his time before he began meeting his public for autographs and photo opportunities. We talked about the city and its continuing economic woes, but Selleck really wanted to speak about his beloved Tigers and their resident slugger at the time by the name of Cecil Fielder. He expanded on how as a boy growing up there he idolized Hall of Fame outfielder Al Kaline.

But then the family moved to Southern California and he was about as far away as he could get from Detroit. He ended up earning a scholarship to play basketball and not baseball at USC thanks in part to his six foot four inch frame. Then as is so often the case of being at the right place at the right time, he was spotted by an acting coach. He made not one, but two appearances on "The Dating Game" while still at Southern Cal and after a very slow beginning, thus began what has proved over time to be a most lucrative career in front of the camera as an actor and behind it as a producer.

And most impressive to me personally is the fact that all the so called "trappings of success" have in no way changed his personality or attitude towards others. Again the word genuine is the best one I can think of to describe Tom Selleck. I also think that characteristic above all others is why he has such a strong following of not only women, but guys like me as well.

THE BAD GUYS

DENNIS CONNER

NOW while I truly have respect for everyone so far that I have written about, these next four individuals I have little if any respect for. I call them the bad guys. And the overall reason for this moniker is what I came across in my dealings with them, some repeatedly. I begin with "Mr. America's Cup", yachtsman Dennis Conner.

If first impressions are an important measure of a person, then it missed the boat (no pun intended) with my visit with Mr. Conner. The first American to lose the famed holy grail of sailing, the America's Cup, and also the first to win it back, was like a light switch in our brief time together. When the camera light was on he was all smiles and pleasant in conversation about his triumphs and failures. Turn the camera off and just like that a one-eighty into a surly, don't bother me attitude.

This event occurred one summer afternoon in 1989 while I was Sports Director at WZZM-TV. Conner was to make a personal appearance in West Michigan and I had been told by the event organizers that he would not be speaking to members of the media afterwards. He was on a very tight schedule to get back to Chicago and wasn't particularly interested in doing so anyway.

Well I am not exactly sure who came up with the idea, but I somehow was able to take a cameraman with me and hitch a ride with representatives of the event on a small private aircraft across Lake Michigan to pick up Conner and bring him to Grand Rapids. The idea was to then to get a few minutes of his time for an interview while on the plane returning back to Michigan. This was after getting an ok from Conner's public relations staff.

So here I am pretty excited about the most unique location I would ever conduct a television interview (aboard an airborne aircraft), but little did I know it would quickly turn to a major disappointment.

We landed in Chicago and almost as soon as the door was opened to the tarmac up the steps strode in Conner and one of his reps. Introductions were quick and just as quickly we were taking off again for the return flight. Conner's man then approached and asked if we were ready to tape and I replied absolutely. We then went over to Conner and with me basically in a kneeling position in the aisle and my cameraman standing above began the interview with Dennis in a seat next to the window. To be clear, until the light actually came on he made no eye contact with either of us or any conversation. But immediately once it was on, he was "on".

For approximately fifteen minutes as he discussed his Olympic Gold Medal in 1976 to his quartet of America's Cup titles and his teams' failure in a bitter loss to the rival Aussies in 1983, it really was pure magic. Conner always had a great looking tan and big smile and it came across exceptionally well on camera. I got a crash course on the incredible amounts of money, time and training it took to be successful in the sport. How it truly was a team effort on and off his craft, the Stars & Stripes. And then it was over.

I had no sooner said "thank you for your time" when Conner quickly turned away and sunk deeply into his seat as if to say "now go away and leave me alone". I didn't even get an extended hand to meet mine for a post interview handshake. My father always said a sign of respect is a firm handshake looking directly at a man with a smile. I got none of that as I pulled my hand back as to not be embarrassed any more than I already was.

I thought maybe I was making too much of it, but my cameraman just shook his head feeling my pain. I got pretty much the same response from the event representatives who could not help but watch and listen in the tight quarters.

Fortunately it was a relatively quick forty-five minute or so flight and once we landed I don't even remember getting off the plane and back to our van for the ride back to the station. I had to be a professional and put together a positive report for the 6 and 11 broadcasts, but deep down I didn't feel good at all about the day's events. I never mentioned this to station management because I had been pleased that they ok'd the trip in the first place, but no completed project before or since left such a bad taste in my mouth.

I did later get some measure of vindication as I heard about another Dennis Conner interview incident. This one involved New Zealand radio and television journalist Sir Paul Holmes the same year I met Conner. Holmes, who passed away in 2013 of cancer, had apparently upset Conner so much so with a question that the skipper just got up and walked out. Years later when it was revealed that Holmes was terminally ill, Conner refused to make peace with the journalist. Holding a grudge seems like one of the many flaws of the man who is also known as "Dirty Dennis".

SCOTT MITCHELL

I have never considered sports to be a life or death proposition. I mean these are games whether on the sandlot or in a packed stadium. I love the competition at any level and always have. However, as a professional athlete who is getting paid to produce most importantly victories, it would seem incumbent to give your best effort every time you step on the field. And afterwards if you did that and still did not come out with a "W" you could feel good about yourself to a certain degree.

That being said, I do find it rather peculiar when say your quarterback, consistently does not seem the least bit upset or remorseful for a poor performance or loss. And that's the bone I always had to pick with former Detroit Lions' Quarterback Scott Mitchell.

The six foot six inch Mitchell came to Detroit as a free agent from the Miami Dolphins after serving several seasons as the back-up to a fella by the name of Marino. Big, strong and with a rocket for a throwing arm, he seemed to be just what the Lions were looking for to compliment and take some pressure off future Hall of Famer Barry Sanders in the backfield. And with receivers such as Herman Moore, Brett Perriman and Johnnie Morton, the offensive balance Head Coach Wayne Fontes was looking for seemed to be heaven sent.

Trouble is, for all the dollars thrown Scott's way by the Honolulu Blue and Silver, he was for all intents and purposes, a non-factor. From 1994 through 1998, he did help lead Detroit to playoff appearances in 1995 and 97, but in both of those playoff games he was quite unspectacular. In the 1995 Wild Card loss at Philadelphia, he had just thirteen completions, a single touchdown and 4 interceptions before being pulled in the second half by Fontes.

I can still see him waving his arms in complete disbelief and saying clearly for everybody to lip read, "Why, why?" Why Scott? It is because you were terrible and the team needed to see if Don Majkowski had any magic left. He tossed a trio of touchdown passes, but the damage was done and it wasn't enough. Then two years later in another Wild Card debacle at Tampa, Mitchell had but ten completions, no touchdowns and another pick.

Even though statistically he had the best season ever for a Lions' quarterback in 1995 in touchdown passes and yards passing which have since been broken, Mitchell in my opinion just never "got it". The game is about the team and he never once that I ever saw took responsibility in some part for any of the regular season or playoff losses.

He had a regular Monday evening appearance on WDIV-TV's sportscast with its' entertaining host Eli Zaret during the regular season. I would always watch to see if after the dust had cleared from the previous day's game what he would have to say for himself. Well, it was almost as if his responses to Eli's questions were scripted. I do not remember ever once him taking individual responsibility for his poor play. It was always "we" need to improve or get better or "we" need to correct our mistakes. It was never "I" need to get better or correct "my" errors. That always bothered me to the point that I lost all respect for him.

It was later reported, though never visually confirmed, that All-Pro Tackle Lomas Brown in Mitchell's first season purposely missed a block that resulted in a game ending injury because he himself was so upset at his quarterback's pathetic play. I don't condone that and I know Lomas I think pretty well and that does not at all sound like something he would ever do. Yet unbelievably I can understand it.

I really don't care what Scott Mitchell's career numbers say (and they are not very good), but I will always question his heart and commitment to the game and his teammates. Following the legendary Bobby Lane in the late 1950's the Detroit Lions had a string of quarterbacks who were something less than spectacular. Had there been even a little of that, his NFL story could have been considerably more positive.

TOM SEAVER

As irritated as I was at Mitchell, I was as just as much shocked at the treatment I received in the Cincinnati Reds dressing room in 1977 just a few weeks after the big trade that brought Cy Young winning pitcher Tom Seaver over from the New York Mets. The same day that Sparky Anderson and I met for the first time and began a longstanding relationship, I went through the single most belittling experience of my career. And remember, technically that career at least professionally, would not begin for another seven years because I was only a collegiate sophomore.

To set the stage, I had just left Sparky's office at Three Rivers Stadium when I spied Seaver alone on the opposite corner of the dressing room near the showers. It was easily several hours prior to game time and I knew that he was not scheduled to pitch that evening so I naturally assumed he would be open to a quick interview. I learned in a New York minute from that point forward to never assume anything.

As I approached Seaver he turned towards me and appeared to be open to a hello. Almost from the first word out of my mouth I began getting F-bombed like never before in my life. "What the "f" do you want? Who the "f" are you? A college kid? Get the "f" outta my face" and he disappeared into another room. This went on for only a few seconds, but it felt like an eternity and I was just left alone standing there and literally shaking. What had I done? Was I missing something? From Tommy Lasorda & Steve Garvey a few months earlier to Sparky just moments before this encounter, I felt I was doing everything properly interview request-wise.

Just then I felt a hand on my right shoulder that snapped me out of my shaking and it turned out to be none other than Pete Rose. That's right, baseball's future all-time hits king and currently still in the midst of a lifetime ban from the game for gambling. But at the moment he was still one of the games' superstars and he said, "Sorry kid. Why don't you head over here with me and some of the other guys and we'd be glad to talk to you."

It turns out Pete was playing cards with a few teammates including Ken Griffey, Sr. and Dan Driessen. Before I knew it I had a tape chock full of members of the "Big Red Machine" all thanks to Rose. I have never forgotten that moment and how a simple act of kindness from Pete helped save me from ending my future career before it really ever started.

Tom "Less than Terrific" Seaver went on to the Hall of Fame while Pete remains in limbo. Now I fully admit I do not agree with or condone his admitted gambling on baseball while still an active player and later as manager of the Reds. But based upon his positive contributions to the game including his outstanding career highlighted by his breaking Ty Cobb's career his record with 4,256, I feel he has more than paid for his crimes. Pete Rose should be reinstated to baseball so he can finally be eligible for and eventually enshrined in Cooperstown. That said I also do not believe he or I will live long enough to ever find out.

As for Tom Seaver, our only common thread since that ill-fated encounter in 1977 is the fact we both contracted Bell's Palsy. This is a disease that causes partial facial paralysis. I don't have any specific information on how Tom's issues have progressed, however, mine are such that since being diagnosed in 2005 I have managed only a fifty percent recovery. That means I cannot fully smile, the left side of my face and eye still droops and my left eye waters excessively when I eat. Other than that I am fine. But it effectively ended my television broadcasting days.

LOU WHITAKER

My final "bad guy" is former Tigers' Second Baseman "Sweet" Lou Whitaker. He clearly did not get that nickname from me. Lou always seemed to have a chip on his shoulder and acted as if the world owed him something. This is a perception I had in my dealings with him and that's really what they were, dealings.

It was never a very comfortable experience to try to get him to talk and when he did it was usually very short and terse. Even in Spring Training where there was always a palpable sense of a fresh start for everybody in the organization, from the players and coaches to even the equipment staff, Whitaker seemed always to be a bit detached and aloof.

And so it was that in the spring of 1989 I was putting together a thirty minute season preview show for WZZM-TV with a format that was going to include an extended sit down interview with Sparky and some feature reports breaking down the club's strengths and possible weaknesses as well as newcomers to the ballclub. The primary feature I and my executive producer wanted was a look back and ahead at the double play tandem of Alan Trammell and Whitaker.

Now mind you, Tram had already done his part with a nice interview and allowing our camera to follow him during workouts including batting practice wearing a microphone to hopefully get some nice candid remarks mixed in. That worked out wonderfully and even though I knew the "live" mic routine likely would be a no go with Lou, at least an actual sit down such as Tram's when the day's workouts were completed, wouldn't be met with a cold no.

Guess what? I went down in flames immediately with my request to Lou. "Man I really don't want to talk about anything." I responded, "But Lou, this is the big feature of our program and would mean so much to us to be able to showcase you guys together." Whitaker didn't acknowledge my statement as he turned and simply walked out of the dressing room.

Things eventually worked out as our planned feature evolved into a slightly different take. We utilized plenty of practice b-roll (video shot by my cameraman that I would voice over) as well as soundbites from Trammell and other players and even some of the fans. I remember being proud of that half hour pre-season show and that feature in particular, considering the changes in it necessitated by the refusal of Lou Whitaker to participate.

You live and learn and I later watched in Lakeland at other Spring Trainings and back in Detroit as writers and broadcasters alike attempted to get comments from Whitaker and most came up empty handed like yours truly.

There was another member of the 1984 World Champion Tigers who did not grant much in the way of interviews and that was veteran outfielder Larry Herndon. But there was a major difference between Larry and Lou. Off camera Larry told me he just felt uncomfortable with that process and I respected him for that as opposed to just "blowing me off". In Whitaker's case, he was simply flat out rude.

I don't recall ever as much as saying another word to him for my remaining time in Michigan. And I cannot but laugh myself when I think back to another Spring Training in Florida where Mitch Album, the popular Detroit sportswriter and author almost came to blows with Whitaker after one of his own ill-fated conversations.

I have always tried to be fair with athletes and coaches I've interviewed with a special emphasis on being "prepared" so that my subjects knew right from the very beginning that I had done my homework. Unfortunately, there are individuals no matter how much you try, who will do everything in their power to be disrespectful to you. I consider myself to be quite lucky that in all my travels only these four men stood out as opposite of what I consider to be "good sports" and "professionals".

THE BROADCASTERS

JIM BRINSON

IN my final career stop at the EMPIRE Sports Network in West Seneca, NY, I met a guy who turned out to be quite simply the most entertaining broadcaster that I have ever met. His name is Jim Brinson.

I eventually became Jim's partner on the late afternoon/early evening edition of FAN-TV as well as Arena Football League telecasts of the Buffalo Destroyers. That team's inaugural coach was another from the Tom Beck coaching tree at Grand Valley State, my longtime close friend, Dave Whinham.

I came to know Jim as a real professional as far as his career was concerned, but away from the spotlight he just made me laugh as few others ever have. He always had a joke or a different spin on things than most others and it always lightened up any situation especially those that can and do occur during "live' telecasts such as FAN-TV.

BOB & JIM BRINSON

No more than 5 feet 6 inches tall and younger looking than he actually is, Jimmy B has one of the greatest set of pipes in the business. I don't know where it comes from, but he obviously has a pair of big ones. And whether doing what he does best which is play-by-play of just about any sport you can think of, or hosting "live" or taped programming, there is nobody better.

He knows his material inside out and is able to infuse every broadcast with his own special brand of humor. One example was in our first year of Arena Football when the Destroyers were on the road in Portland, Oregon. Jim's partner that first year in 1999 was former NFL linebacker Ray Bentley who would eventually take over as head coach in Buffalo. But Jim and Ray were like those old characters from Sesame Street sitting up in the theater box, Statler and Waldorf on any given telecast. Instead of the theater box, they were in the press box calling the games and making fun of me as the "sideline" reporter at every opportunity.

Of course I gave them plenty of material to work with like that game in Portland. During a break I grabbed a couple of hot dogs to scarf down since I had worked up an appetite bouncing all over the arena for different reports. Well the knucklehead that I am didn't select a suitable out of sight location to eat and sure enough the camera focused a shot of me eating and Jim and Ray took no mercy, just laughing it up at my expense on "live" television. I will never live that one down.

I probably had more fun doing those Destroyers games for five seasons than any other assignment I ever took part in during my career. And I owe most of that to my partner and friend, Jim Brinson. Just turn on your television or radio and chances are you'll still see or hear those golden pipes anywhere from Buffalo to Tucson, from Little Rock to Des Moines. And in the words of Jimmy B,"Break it down for us."

JACK BUCK

There is another broadcaster with the initials "JB" that more of the American sports public likely has heard of and that man is the late Jack

Buck. The longtime voice of the St. Louis Cardinals was also well versed in most any other professional sport and I had the opportunity to meet him for the first time in Pittsburgh at Three Rivers Stadium for a regionally televised CBS broadcast featuring the host Steelers. Jack was calling the action that day with his partner Hank Stram, the former Head Coach of the Kansas City Chiefs whom he led to victory in Super Bowl 4 over the Vikings. A few hours before kickoff he took time to give a young sportscaster a few pointers as well as some great advice.

"Bob, you cannot get a job in this business until you get experience and you can't get experience until you get a job. Once you figure that out everything else should fall into place as long as you are persistent and always doing your best and listening to direction." Mr. Buck was so sincere and I definitely took it to heart and always tried to live up to that sound advice. He was like a grandfather passing down his years of experience. He knew I appreciated our limited time together and that in itself was something that left a lasting impression on me.

Today his son Joe is well known to this generation of sports fans on FOX for NFL Telecasts and MLB Post Season Play including the World Series. And while I never made it to the network level myself except for some limited sideline NFL reporting also for FOX, I know that my time in the business was helped without question by the words of wisdom and experience of Jack Buck whom I consider one of the top sports broadcasters ever.

CURT GOWDY

A contemporary of the elder Buck who himself is considered to be one of the most revered sportscasters of all-time is the legendary Curt Gowdy. And like my meeting with Jack Buck, my introduction to Mr. Gowdy also occurred at Three Rivers Stadium for yet another Steelers telecast. This one was on NBC with Curt paired with his longtime partner and former NFL player Al DeRogatis.

Curt Gowdy was a part of some of the biggest events in sports history while at the mic, calling the action of Super Bowl 3 and Joe Namath's Jets upsetting the heavily favored Baltimore Colts. He was also front and center for what I and many others believe to be the most exciting World Series ever played, the 1975 epic showdown between Boston and Cincinnati.

Gowdy's advice was similar to Buck's, but at the same time with a slightly different spin. He said, "Find a radio or tv station anywhere in America to get your foot in the door. Get air-time, practice and develop a style of your own. Make your mistakes in smaller markets and then work your way up. Then, and most importantly, find a market or city that you want to work in and put down roots if possible. This business has a tendency to create gypsies. You get to where you want to be then think you want to go someplace else."

As I look back I did exactly what he said to do except for the part of putting down roots. My roots lasted about six or seven years in one market then I felt it was time to move on and up. I never made it to my ultimate goal which was to be on the air in my hometown Pittsburgh market. I guess that's why I kept working towards getting home.

ERNIE HARWELL

Without question the most beloved broadcaster I got to meet and become friends with was the late voice of the Detroit Tigers, Mr. Ernie Harwell. Just closing my eyes I can still hear his southern drawl with his signature call for a home run,"And it's long gone".

Ernie took over Tigers' broadcasts in 1960 and also was utilized on national radio and television baseball events throughout his tenure in Detroit. He was an integral part of that original group of broadcasters like Red Smith, Mel Allen and Vin Scully who were among the first to bring baseball to us in a most personal and stylish way. Ernie became as much a recognized and revered part of the team as the players themselves. A statue of him graces the entrance of Comerica Park in the Motor City as a tribute to his indelible mark on the franchise.

ERNIE HARWELL & BOB at Spring Training in Lakeland, FL

I get chills each time I play back a tape of his famous poem about the game he loved with one verse in particular. "In baseball, democracy shines its clearest. Here the only race that matters is the race to the bag. The creed is the rulebook. Color is only something to distinguish one team's uniform from another."

I had the chance to sit down with Ernie and visit him in press boxes from Lakeland, Florida to Anaheim, California and of course his perch inside old Tiger Stadium. Along with his partner, the late Paul Carey (who by the way was as close to the voice of God himself as any human being who ever lived), they painted a picture of the game that was as complete and convincing to give you the feeling you were sitting right there in the stands. For boys and girls, men and women, they got their Tigers' action from Ernie and Paul whether in their cars or homes or businesses and all was right with the world.

PAUL CAREY, BOB & ERNIE HARWELL

When I left Detroit under less than perfect circumstances in 1998 and called Ernie to simply say "thank you" for his friendship, advice and positive influence, I did not get just a kind word. I was invited to join him and his lovely wife Lulu along with my wife and sons for a visit to his home for an afternoon to talk baseball. Those few hours sitting in his den and watching as he drew the kids into story after story about the game and its tradition will never leave me.

I believe baseball more than any other team sport in this country is perpetuated by that tradition and the players that came before the current crop of talent. And though I always gave the kids my take on such things when we would sit together at ballparks all over this country, it was apparent that when in the presence of a master storyteller like Ernie, the message came through much more loud and clear.

It's a prime reason I am convinced today that those three young men enjoy "America's Pastime" as deeply as they do. I sincerely thank you Ernie. That was your gift to me and my boys that will live within us forever.

BILL HILLGROVE

Home in Western Pennsylvania there have been many broadcasters for me to admire with "The Gunner" Bob Prince of the Pirates my favorite growing up. "Chicken on the Hill with Will" (The call for slugger Willie Stargell after he stroked a homer that would mean free chicken to whomever was at the checkout of his restaurant at that moment),"We need a hoover" (a double play) and the "Green Weenie" (a plastic pickle shaped toy that would put the whammy on the opposition shaken in unison). These were ways Bob got us involved in his broadcasts of the exploits of Willie and Roberto and Maz and the rest of our Buccos.

Today on the football side of things as he has for several decades, Steelers' fans are blessed to have a voice of equal enthusiasm in the person of Bill Hillgrove. Bill took over for the late Jack Fleming and originally partnered with a real Pittsburgh icon, the late Myron Cope.

BILL HILLGROVE & BOB

I first met Bill in Athens, Ohio while still in college and he was in town to call the basketball contest between my Bobcats and his Pitt Panthers. Bill has what you might conclude is a rather busy schedule with Pitt hoops and football along with the Steelers. He always has had a wonderful sense of humor about most things, especially his ability to get from one location to another when both his NFL and college responsibilities are intertwined in the same weekend.

You will not find a nicer, more laid back personality than Bill's and that is his major strength I think on his broadcasts. He sounds like one of us, as if we are the storyteller of the game action. So there is a kinship that has developed over these many years and Bill is as much a part of the Pittsburgh and Western Pennsylvania sports scene as any player or coach.

I had the pleasure of lining Bill up as a pre-game guest for insights on what to expect on the upcoming game between say Pitt and visiting Syracuse at old Pitt Stadium as well as much the same at Heinz Field prior to a Steelers-Bills matchup.

I truly appreciated Bill Hillgrove and his voice over the years while living in Ohio, then Michigan and finally New York where my career path took me. Watching hometown highlights from other markets brought me closer to where I grew up and thanks to Bill, closing my eyes it was as if I never left.

MIKE LANGE

The Steel City's other legendary voice is that of the Penguins' Mike Lange. Long before there was Chris Berman on ESPN, Mike was the voice with the most notoriety for signature catch phrases that were repeated by fans not only in Pittsbugh, but throughout the country.

"Scratch my back with a hacksaw", "Michael, Michael motorcycle" , "He beat him like a rented mule", "Buy Sam a drink and get his dog one too" and the most famous of all, "Heeeeeeeeeeeeeee shoots and scores". These are some of Mike's endless pocketbook of sayings to emphasize

Pens' goals or what a Pittsburgh player did to an unfortunate opponent and are etched in my mind now and forever.

Incredibly, even more than Bill Hillgrove with the Steelers, Mike IS Pittsburgh Penguins hockey as far as I am concerned. Since 1974 when he first became the play-by-play man for the team, Mike has entrenched himself in the hearts and minds of fans young and old. First on television and now on radio, he has an extremely unique way of describing the action on the ice and does so with a passion that is unequaled.

BOB & MIKE LANGE

From my college days getting press passes to Pittsburgh games at the Civic Arena which eventually became Mellon Arena, I spent many an afternoon or evening in the Igloo's press box high above the action. Either practicing my own play-by-play skills or sitting behind Mike and his string of color analysts, it was an education that you could only get at the game itself as opposed to a classroom. The arena was my classroom and in this case the professor was Mike Lange.

Years later when I had established my career, I would utilize my connection with him to get pre-game insights much like Hillgrove's. Most notably those came with the EMPIRE Sports Network where we had all the regular season and first round playoff series telecasts and plenty of air time to fill. Mike was always happy to help in any way he could when he and the Penguins were in town and showed me what a true professional is in a business that does not always produce such gentlemen.

I specifically remember setting up outside Mellon Arena in the 1999 playoffs as the Sabres and our crew came to town and had to produce a multitude of pre-game "live" shots inside of FAN-TV prior to each contest. We were able to corral just about every sportswriter and tv and radio personality in Pittsburgh from Stan Savran and Alby Oxenreiter to Joe Starkey and Mike Prisuta for their take on the series and the matchups.

But Mike always stood head and shoulders above the rest and honestly in over twenty years behind the mic myself, I never received a compliment that meant as much as Mike's. He exuded his feelings on "live" television about what EMPIRE and I specifically brought in the form of the most complete programming before and after the Buffalo games all season long. It was his belief that the rest of the NHL's franchises could learn a thing or two from us about covering and promoting the league and the team. It was certainly high praise from a man I had admired since I was a youngster and it sure gave me confidence that what we were doing at EMPIRE was on the money.

RAY LANE

In the fall of 1991 I finally made it to the "big time" with my move to Detroit and WKBD-TV. At the time we were the FOX Network affiliate and the ninth largest market in the country. That meant there were a heckuva lot of viewers each evening for our hour long Ten o'clock news/ weather & sports. It was in this environment that I thrived under the wisdom and guidance of Sports Director Ray Lane.

Affectionately known as "The Doctor", Ray was a friend to all and outside of Ernie Harwell I know of no one else in the business that was as universally respected. He was the perfect ying to my yang, the Batman to my Robin. An old and wily veteran who'd seen and done it all coupled with a young and enthusiastic newcomer who definitely needed to be reined in at times.

RAY LANE & BOB

Ray had a sense of humor that was priceless and an ability to get the most out of any interview subject he had. As the pre-game, between periods and post- game host of our Detroit Red Wings telecasts he had plenty of practice. From players to coaches and general managers, "Doctor" Lane had the perfect prescription for insightful and thoughtful responses from his guests. Our Executive Producer Toby Cunningham was blessed not only with Ray, but play-by-play voice Dave Strader and former Wings' player Mickey Redmond adding commentary.

It was an all-star team and I was excited beyond belief to be a small part of that package with my own pre and post- game features and wrap-up reports. That experience served me well for my next stop in Buffalo where EMPIRE took what we did in Detroit to a whole new level if for no other reason than sheer air-time.

Ray made everybody feel important from producers, directors, tape editors and even interns. Anyone involved at WKBD was never left out. He demonstrated on a daily basis what my own father had tried to instill in me growing up. And whether it was in the studio just before a telecast or deep in the bowels of Joe Louis Arena watching the action on the ice with our feed into the dressing room we used as our between periods interviews, Ray could have us all in stitches nearly in tears laughing so hard at one of his quips or stories. That's why I call Ray,"Doctor" Lane, because I almost needed stitches after busting a gut at one of his tales.

As I have stated several times earlier, I left Detroit because of butting heads with my news director. But I will never have anything but positive memories of my time there thanks to my friend and mentor Ray Lane. We remain friends to this day and I treasure our regular phone conversations. I toast you Ray to our many happy days together in the Motor City.

RAY SCOTT

The "other" Ray that influenced my career was the man whom I credit with giving me the notion of doing what he did for a career in the first place. I mean I could always talk. And talk and talk. I would entertain my aunts and uncles and cousins with the impressions I did at family gatherings, so I was comfortable at a very early age getting up in front of people. But I was most interested in, if not playing or watching sports, then talking about sports. And my earliest recollections on television are of the glory days of the Green Bay Packers and their national telecasts on CBS.

Ray Scott was the voice that struck a chord in me with a most succinct description of the game action. I can still hear as clear as if it was only yesterday, "Starr, Taylor, touchdown Packers." Ray was there for the "Ice Bowl" as well as Super Bowls I and II with Vince Lombardi and company and would later move on to play-by-play duties with the expansion Tampa Bay Buccaneers and finally the Minnesota Vikings.

He also dabbled in college football and it was there on the campus of Penn State in 1979 that I first got to meet him. It was a breakfast conversation between another professor and an eager student as Ray was preparing for his telecast later that afternoon on the TCS Sports Network based in New Kensington, a Pittsburgh suburb. Ray partnered with George Paterno, the brother of longtime Nittany Lions' patriarch, the late Joe Paterno on those telecasts.

My dad always told me that nobody was going to give me anything in this life. If I wanted something I would have to find a way and go out and get it and that is exactly how my morning get together with Ray Scott happened. I had written him a personal letter and found a way to get his home address in Edina, Minnesota telling him of my career aspirations and that he was my model to try and emulate. Not only did I surprisingly get a hand written response, but that invite to meet in State College when I had advised him of a road trip to campus with friends from Pittsburgh for the Pitt-Penn State game. I still have those letters and correspondence to this day.

From our first handshake and through more letters (no cell phones in those days) and another face to face in the press box at Anaheim Stadium for a Vikings-Rams game, Ray made me feel as though I had some tangible ability and always took a genuine interest in where my career travels had taken me. He was the first person to help validate what I was trying to accomplish in broadcasting and was nothing but positive.

It was a sad day when I learned of his passing in March of 1998. And the irony there is that his death came just fifteen days after the passing of my favorite Green Bay Packer of all-time, linebacker Ray Nitschke. The year following Gale Sayers induction into the Pro Football Hall of Fame I was once again on hand for the 1978 ceremony predominately because of the old Packer warrior's own induction.

Old number 66 was so beloved in retirement that after he passed away, the annual pre-induction luncheon where the new inductees dined with the greats already enshrined, was named in his honor.

So for whatever I actually did accomplish in my career, I am indebted to Mr. Ray Scott for helping me to believe in myself. His lasting advice was, "Always be yourself Bob. Take bits and pieces of what you like that a particular broadcaster does and incorporate that into your own skills and style. Be positive, be honest and again above all, be yourself." I can only hope that from Kalamazoo to Lansing to Toledo to Grand Rapids to Detroit to Buffalo and everywhere in between, that viewers found me to be honest and myself.

JIM TICHEY

My first full time job in broadcasting came in Toledo, Ohio at the ABC station, WDHO-TV. After getting my feet wet as a part timer in Lansing, Michigan it was time to get a full time gig and thanks to some good tape and an interview that was to me the best of any I had ever done, I was selected to be the Weekend Sports Anchor & Weekday Sports Reporter. My first Sports Director was Jim Tichey, who like Ray Lane in Detroit, was a longtime established part of the Northwest Ohio sports scene.

And like Ray, Jim could not have been a nicer and easy going man to work with. Even after I committed a most embarrassing behind the scenes mistake, "Tich" found it in his heart to forgive me. Almost. You see in those days we worked with three quarter inch big and bulky tape where we stored our sportscasts, feature stories and music. Jim was a fanatic about his instrumental music to utilize when needed as background.

BOB & JIM TICHEY

So on this particular day I had come back from shooting a story for the six and eleven o'clock sports segment. I would edit my own video and interviews and stand-up into a finished feature (two different versions) lasting no longer than a minute and forty five seconds each. To this day I simply cannot explain what happened next other than to say I was obviously not paying attention. I grabbed a tape to record the feature on and did not pay attention to the fact it was Jim's master music tape.

Years, yes years, of music he had collected was on that tape which inexplicably had somehow found its' way onto a pile of other reusable tapes. Should I have looked at the box cover? Yes. Did I? No. The rest is history. The features were fine and Tich even complimented me on them which I only remember because later the next day he found them smack dab in the middle of his music library.

He had every right to be ticked off and for a short time he sure was. I was speechless. I apologized and learned a very hard lesson about paying attention to what I was doing that I never let happen again.

Unlike those infamous missing eighteen minutes from President Nixon's White House recordings during the Watergate era, there was nothing missing here, just covered up. Did I just say that? But that one negative incident has never left me because I still feel horrible that it happened.

It eventually became a mere blemish really in the long run in Toledo and Tich and I remain friends. It was great working with him and without question helped prepare me for what was ahead. I will always appreciate Jim Tichey and remember our big advertising billboard (Tichey N Trimble,"TNT" Dynamite Sports Coverage You Can Count On).

THE RACERS

MARIO ANDRETTI

I have always been a fan of motor sports, but growing up in Western Pennsylvania the closest I ever got to an actual race was on my television. Whether it was the Indianapolis 500 or a NASCAR event I was a mere spectator from the comfort of my parents' living room.

Of course that all changed once my broadcast career began in Michigan. And one name above all others for me personally was synonymous with speed and that name was Mario Andretti.

From the time I saw Mario win his one any only Indy 500 in 1969 I was hooked on the Indy Car circuit. Seeing him celebrate with that big smile in victory lane alongside his team owner Andy Granatelli and the STP Oil Treatment commercials that followed, it was a turning point in my interest in the sport. And you could not ask for a better role model than Mario. Whether Indy Cars, NASCAR or Formula One and beyond, the little Italian was and is the standard to be measured by. If not for his 109 wins worldwide in major events, then for the professional way he conducted and still conducts himself as the greatest ambassador racing has ever known.

During each and every stop in my career except the last one at EMPIRE, I regularly covered racing from the short track Berlin Raceway near Grand Rapids to the famed Brickyard itself in Indianapolis. And it was in Gasoline Alley of the famed Indianapolis Motor Speedway that I first encountered Mario Andretti.

MARIO ANDRETTI & BOB

Covering Amway sponsored driver Scott Brayton whom I will profile next, I was afforded the opportunity to spend several days each May for practice sessions early in the month. At Indy in the month of May you are smack dab in the epicenter of the finest open wheeled racing talent, sponsorship and ownership on the planet. And Mario at that time in the late 1980's was still driving in his fifties, currently for the Newman-Haas Team.

It was Mario, after Scott initially, that really introduced me to the behind the scenes world of racing. From the development of the engine and the painstaking attention to detail for each and every component in a race car, Mario gave me a personal education that was every bit as entertaining as it was informative. Being in the various garages in Gasoline Alley where the cars are prepared and tweaked for the days and nights leading up to race day was just fascinating.

MARIO ANDRETTI & BOB

And while the majority of "tech speak" went right over my head I was witness to the type of passion that each and every successful person I have every met in my life demonstrated. To be the best you must work. And work and then when you are really tired and ready to shut it down for the day, work some more.

Even more successful as a businessman than he ever was on tracks from Indiana to Monaco, Mario Andretti is simply one of the best ever at what he sets his mind to.

SCOTT BRAYTON

One thing that I do not miss about my career covering auto racing is the way the sport can in an instant take away the life of a human being. There were men that I considered at the very least interview subjects and at most, close friends.

I had the pleasure of talking to a pair of budding NASCAR superstars and then Alan Kulwicki and Davey Allison were gone. And Rich Vogler, not really a household name in the sport but a man that would drive on anything from dirt tracks in the country way off the beaten path to Indy. Then he too was gone. That is what made the sudden passing of my pal Scott Brayton on May 17, 1996 almost unbearable to accept.

Scott had just won the pole for the upcoming Indy 500 the previous week when during a practice run in his backup car he had a rear tire blowout going into turn two on the short chute. So at over 200 miles per hour his car and head slammed into the wall. In that instant my thirty seven year old friend was dead. His spirit and smile though are a constant image in the back of my mind that I will never forget.

Since coming to Grand Rapids where the Amway Corporation was founded and based, I was immediately immersed in the company's sponsorship and promotion of its Indy Car program. Public Relations man Bob Johnson was in charge of getting local sports media types such as me from television, radio and the Grand Rapids Press together. And each spring we took off for a flight to Indianapolis aboard a ridiculously spacious private Amway jet for the less than one hour flight for a few days at the track. We had virtually unlimited access to watch Scott and his crew prepare for what announcer Paul Page aptly dubbed, "The Greatest Spectacle in Racing" each Memorial Day weekend.

SCOTT BRAYTON & BOB

Scott and I developed a real friendship over several years and especially on these trips did we connect and converse about much more than racing. Amway's staff always treated us first class and besides the days at the track, the evenings at one of the great steakhouses in the nation, St. Elmo's, were even more special to me.

Located in the heart of the city, it featured walls covered with photos of its famous patrons from Mike Phipps, the great college quarterback from Purdue, to a who's who of racing types who conducted their business a few miles to the west in Speedway, Indiana. Besides those mouthwatering steaks let me tell you, you will never, ever have a bigger or spicier shrimp cocktail anywhere.

Scott and former WOTV-TV Sport Director Warren Reynolds along with Bob Johnson used to giggle almost uncontrollably as I, (not a spicy food fan at all) because of the unrelenting peer pressure, would proceed to dip my shrimp into that St. Elmo's fire breathing cocktail sauce. There was simply not enough ice water in the city to chill my taste buds and Scott got the biggest kick out of that.

BOB & SCOTT BRAYTON

Then one year we got a surprise. After dinner we would all jump into a couple of vans for about an hour's drive north towards Kokomo for an evening of go-kart racing. Now Scott and I were the last to walk out of the restaurant and he offered to drive me up in his Camaro. So I took a milli-second to accept. The choice, a van stuffed to capacity with friends from the media, OR a solo drive with an active Indy car racer? I chose the latter and it proved just incredible. Scott's girlfriend and future wife Becky called while on the way up and he passed the phone over for me to say hello and I will never forget her words. "Just take care of my baby, don't embarrass him on the track and bring him back in one piece, ok Bob?" I laughed and said no problem.

But the laughing stopped a few years later on that horrific weekend in 1996 when Scott lost his life. You see I had spoken by phone to Scott to congratulate him on winning his second Indy pole only a few days earlier and when I was checking the wire for the latest sports updates and spotted the news of his crash I felt like I had been punched in the stomach.

I know I collapsed against the wall and my eyes started watering. Co-workers came rushing to me to see what was wrong and just about everybody including the evening's producer said just forget about the show. They would figure things out and for me just to take as much time as I needed to pull myself together and then just go home. But I could not do that.

I had a responsibility to them and myself and with a very heavy heart I went on as planned, but to this day do not in any way shape or form remember doing so. I was in a fog for the next few days and did take an excused day to attend Scott's funeral service in his hometown of Coldwater, Michigan.

Many of his racing contemporaries including drivers, crewmen, owners and media members came to offer their condolences and I have but one lasting image of that day. Atop his coffin was the helmet he was wearing when the crash occurred. There were no cracks or anything except a single scratch mark on the right upper portion of it where obviously his head took the brunt of the force when hitting the retaining wall.

I miss Scott and his outgoing personality. And I am proud for him to have considered me to be his friend as Becky told me following the service. It meant a great deal to me then and now.

A.J. FOYT

In a business where speed and power are both necessary to be successful, nobody personified both traits in and out of a race car like Anthony Joseph Foyt, Jr. The first four time winner of the Indianapolis 500 was a strong willed and determined Texan who idolized his father and who worked with him to develop one of the most tenacious competitors any sport has ever known.

During my first trip to Indy as part of Amway's "Brayton Bunch" I had the chance to get up close and personal with A.J. in his normal racing surroundings. It had been over 8 years since we first met in Kalamazoo, Michigan where his main sponsor, Jim Gilmore, resided and had his business headquarters.

At the time I was in my first post-college job as the Ice Events Coordinator at Wings Stadium, the home to the Kalamazoo Wings of the International Hockey League.

Ted and Martha Parfet of the Upjohn Corporation were the primary owners of the Wings' franchise, with Mr. Gilmore owning a minority stake himself. I was introduced to them by the Wings' Head Coach and General Manager Bob Lemieux who also happened to be the man who hired me out of Ohio University.

It sure is strange how things come full circle in life sometimes. I went to school and graduated with a communications degree, but began my post-college days nowhere near a press box or microphone. Instead I was selling ice time and sharpening skates at the stadium. But Bob knew of my career plans and always made it a point to introduce me to people and eventually those Kalamazoo introductions paid off as a broadcaster.

You see Bob's lovely wife Mariette was Jim Gilmore's Executive Assistant, and once I returned to West Michigan at WZZM-TV, I asked Mariette for a favor. I wanted to see if through Mr. Gilmore he could advise A.J. of my coming to Indy and if he would be able to make time to see me for an interview. The stars aligned and the at times gruff Mr. Foyt was like a teddy bear allowing my cameraman and me access inside his garage. Streaming fans could only watch from behind the temporary retaining fence as A.J. leaned against a rack of tires with his arms folded across his thick chest and proceeded to answer every one of my questions.

It was interesting to hear him recall his father and the love he had for his "daddy" as he referred to him as a man himself in his fifties at the time. His father taught him to be self-sufficient and tough and those traits served him quite well during his illustrious racing career. To this day he is still the only driver in history to win the Indy 500, the Daytona 500, the 24 Hours of Daytona and the 24 Hours of Le Mans.

I would label A.J. just as an intimidating a presence as Mike Ditka in his respective sport. The primary difference between the two men to me though is that Iron Mike always seemed to be approachable away from the field. Foyt didn't appear to be that way at all, purposefully keeping people at an arm's length until he discovered their motives.

I related this feeling I had towards him in the garage that day and he got a good sized Texas laugh about it. And after that in several other meetings or interviews I never felt that way again because A.J. put that guard down and trusted me.

It is another one of those minor regrets that I have to this day, the inability to be as close to the drivers as I once was. I truly miss the combination of their varied personalities, the smell of ethanol and the real excitement and anticipation in the air around the track on race day. In a word, it is absolutely "intoxicating". And I will always appreciate that tough Texan A.J. Foyt for being a big part of that picture.

RICK MEARS

Of all the many race drivers I have had the pleasure of meeting my unquestioned favorite is Rick Mears. Like A.J., Rick is also a four time winner of the Indianapolis 500, but he did so in such a low key and what appeared to be effortless way that many fans and observers thought it unusual if Rick did not win a race.

He was just smooth in everything he did in a race car. And in many conversations with him from the Old Brickyard in Indianapolis to the Irish Hills of Southeast Michigan at Michigan international Speedway, Rick was a real gem. He was exceptionally friendly to me while at the same time quite humble about his own accomplishments. He was always quick to point out the hard work of his crew and the leadership of his friend and team owner Roger Penske.

ROGER PENSKE & RICK MEARS

During the 1980's and 90's in the years I covered the Indy Car circuit, "Team Penske" was a continually evolving all-star parade of drivers that were some of the finest the sport has ever seen. Besides Mears, Roger was able to secure the services of such elite drivers as Al Unser, Emerson Fittipaldi, Danny Sullivan, Al Unser Jr and Paul Tracy among them. And while each of those men captured at least one Indy crown (Al Unser, Sr. with a quartet as has Foyt and Mears) except for Tracy, it is Rick Mears who set the standard for Penske Racing in his distinctive Pennzoil yellow car.

RICK MEARS & BOB

As most drivers, Rick had his share of racing mishaps with the two biggest coming in a pit fire at the 1981 Indy race where he received severe facial burns. Then in the second half of the 1984 season where he earlier had captured his second Indianapolis 500, he suffered horrific leg injuries most notably to his right foot. It is that incident that physically plagued him for really the rest of his driving days.

Rick was very candid about any aspect of his career when we spoke and the injuries I know specifically hurried his retirement from the sport. While elder contemporaries such as Andretti and Foyt raced well into their fifties, Mears said enough was enough at just forty one.

He accomplished far more than he ever anticipated he would behind the wheel and since stepping away as an active driver, he has served as an extremely valued consultant to Team Penske. I cannot think of a finer person or teacher to the new breed of racer than Rick Mears.

ROGER PENSKE

Just as I admire Rick Mears as the finest driver I ever saw, Roger Penske is the standard as a team owner and quite frankly businessman I have ever known. I remember making the statement to him one time that I nicknamed him "recession proof" and proceeded to explain why and I think I took him aback because of my sincere admiration.

As a team owner and the head of Penske Enterprises he has a hand in so many different business ventures it is just mind boggling. All are related to the automobile industry and all are wildly successful. And therein stands my statement about being recession proof. Roger has a gift. His gift is recognizing talent, be it a race car driver or an engineer or marketing strategist.

BOB & ROGER PENSKE

His philosophy is straightforward in the business world. Using Penske Racing as an example he says, "I will always treat you with respect, I will provide you with the best research and equipment and I will compensate you better than anyone else. What I ask in return is a 100% effort at all times and most importantly, results."

It is hard to argue with that success. As of this writing Roger remains the winningest team owner in Indianapolis 500 history with sixteen Borg-Warner trophies. It is also hard to argue that another big reason he is universally revered in the business world, is that he really is a very down to earth nice guy. Away from the pressures of the board room where his decisions affect the lives of thousands of employees worldwide, he is incredibly approachable.

In all my conversations and attempts to set up interviews either well in advance or even at the last second, Roger always seemed to somehow make time for me. We talked in Gasoline Alley at Indy, on Pit Row at Michigan International Speedway, in his air conditioned trailer on Belle Isle for the Detroit Grand Prix. Even at the Holiday Inn in East Grand Rapids where he had his own speaking engagement in between my 6 and 11pm sports reports on WZZM. I will always respect Roger Penske for that.

I feel that I must have been doing something right during those years to have one of the most powerful and successful businessmen in the United States think enough of me to take time out of his frantic schedule on a fairly regular basis.

BOBBY RAHAL

Another successful businessman following a strong professional racing career is Bobby Rahal. The 1986 Indy 500 champion as a driver and 2004 champ as an owner, Bobby won three Indy Car season championships which are testaments to his talent and consistency behind the wheel.

We spoke often during the 80's and 90's trackside, and my favorite memories are really informal chats away from the camera's eye at a Go Kart track a few miles away from Michigan International Speedway.

Marlboro Team Penske Public Relations Chief Brian Muir came up with a neat idea. He was able to set up an afternoon of racing between members of the media such as myself and a select group of Indy Car drivers. This was a regular pre-race routine for several years in the late 80's and early 90's.

I always brought along my wife and two young sons at the time to enjoy the festivities which included racing, then lunch and then interviews before heading back to Detroit. The kids loved seeing their dad get buckled up for a few laps around the road course that had twists and turns and a big drop and tight corner to negotiate right after the green flag. Bobby himself loved taking part along with drivers such as Al Unser, Jr., Robby Gordon, Paul Tracy, Christian Fittipaldi, and Adrian Fernandez among others.

And credit Rick Mears for regularly being in attendance, but merely as a spectator. His aforementioned foot injuries made it uncomfortable to do so, especially with novices like myself as competition.

Now I'd like to think I am a pretty competitive person and with my wife and kids watching as well as my own inner drive, I really wanted once to be the media winner of this event. Keys to victory, follow the line set up on the track by the pros and avoid contact with another driver because even a little bump can throw you off that line and add seconds to your run. Bobby always gave me some pointers and I tried to follow them to the letter. Trouble is, there was one driver who seemed to have it out for me. His name was Robby Gordon.

I'd interviewed Robby several times over the years and found him to be a really good kid. He was young and hungry, but had developed a reputation for making contact with other drivers and so he wasn't the most popular guy on the circuit with several very public run ins with other drivers. And on this day I found that out first hand.

Somehow I was lucky enough to draw the pole position in the formation. Five rows of two and here was Trimble with what appeared to be a gift not to be wasted. I received final instructions from Coach Rahal, a handshake and we were off and running.

Leading the field to that first dip in the course that took us hard to the left then right up the hill, I never made it that far. Gordon had managed in just seconds to get around a trio of cars and was right on my tail. He then veered to his right, got alongside me, smiled and drove me into the wall for a sudden and hard stop that really did jerk my neck pretty good. As he waved his arm in a bye- bye motion I was left behind watching everyone pass me, my go-kart done for the day.

It's sad I know, but I was really more than angry. I wanted a chance to win and finally take home this awesome black leather and cloth Marlboro Team Penske jacket that goes to the victor each year. I do not, nor have I ever smoked cigarettes, but the jacket was very cool and I could see myself wearing it on days in the cold Michigan winters. But, it was not to be.

Rahal was the first to greet me when I got back to the start finish line and said Gordon absolutely did that on purpose, but that was racing, even in this environment. Robby did come up to me after the race and offer an apology, but the look I gave him probably said more than any words could as I simply walked away.

The next year at the event which proved to be the final one, Bobby was the first driver I saw and before I could say a word I was just shocked that he actually remembered the Gordon incident and he asked how I was feeling. That said a lot to me about Rahal. Again, here is this professional driver and businessman with a million things on his mind and he still was thoughtful enough to remember what had happened a full year earlier. Thanks Bobby. That meant a lot to me.

DANNY SULLIVAN

The poster boy for the Indy Car circuit with movie star looks in the mid to late 1980's was Danny Sullivan. Another one of the stable of stars for Team Penske, Danny really burst onto the national scene with his incredible spin and win at the 1985 Indianapolis 500.

Even if you are not a follower of the sport or a racing fan, I am sure you've seen the footage from that ABC telecast. After just passing Mario Andretti on the 120th lap, he did a complete 360 spin, somehow regained control and righted himself and eventually went on to victory. It is singularly for me the most defining moment of any race I have ever seen. And while it would be some three years after that event that I first met Danny, he was more than happy to relive that moment for me in the first of many interviews over the next several years.

Like so many aspiring actors who have told stories of waiting tables while looking for their break into acting, Sullivan's story was somewhat similar. After lumberjacking and cab driving, he finally got a shot at driving a race car professionally. He persevered and that old adage of being at the right place at the right time paid off. He was able to secure a ride first in Europe and then back here in the United States before that May day in 1985 that changed his life.

DANNY SULLIVAN & BOB

But unlike another media darling, Danica Patrick, who was beautiful and a Madison Avenue goldmine with advertising opportunities, Danny actually went on to a solid career. He finished up with seventeen Indy Car victories including the 1988 Michigan 500 at MIS. Danica might have "Go Daddy" on her resume, but she has never actually gone to the winners circle in a professional race. Sullivan was like Rick Mears in the respect that he made what he did look easy. Of course, I know that what these professionals do and the risks they take are anything but easy.

And what they do including those risks are what make them special and admired. In fact one year at Indy while shooting some footage of Danny and his crew during a practice session, actress Whoopie Goldberg arrived behind us very unsuspecting and caught Danny's eye.

He hurdled the retaining wall and they spoke for several minutes as we moved out of the way and it was readily apparent that these two had a lot in common. They were stars in their own right, both instantly recognizable and hounded by adoring fans. Yet in those minutes they looked extremely comfortable talking as friends without any outside celebrity pressures.

Like the other drivers I have spoken about, Danny Sullivan was all class and somewhat surprised at the success he had attained to that point. Also like Mears he was quick to point out the tremendous efforts of his team and humbled by the notoriety he had attained as a result of his success.

AL UNSER, JR.

The final driver I want to talk about is Al Unser, Jr. "Little Al" is the son of four time Indianapolis 500 winner Al Unser, Sr. and nephew of an Indy 500 winner himself, Bobby Unser. But make no mistake, Junior was every bit a champion driver in his own right as he has a pair of Indy 500 victories to his credit as well.

Being born into a racing family brought with it certain pressures and expectations that might have turned him in another direction if he did not have the same passion for the sport. But that was not the case for this Al as he strove like his rival in their racing heyday, Mario's son Michael Andretti, to become one of the premier drivers on the Indy Car circuit.

When you combine his victory totals in the CART and IRL series he amassed thirty-four checkered flags over his career. That once again demonstrated what makes the difference between good and great in any sport. Consistency.

Like the previous drivers I have talked about, Little Al was deeply involved in the set-up of his car. And not coincidentally because of his family and background, he knew as much about the nuts and bolts of his cars as he did when he got behind the wheel. And this is the time when I knew him, stepping out of the shadow of his father and uncle to not only become a championship caliber driver, but one of the series' most popular attractions.

BOB & AL UNSER JR.

"Little Al" would take part in our go-kart races each year in Michigan leading up to the Michigan 500. More than any of the drivers I met and interviewed over the years, he always recognized me and never turned down an interview request. Following his retirement Al would find difficulties adjusting as he battled alcoholism and several very public DUI incidents involving his personal vehicles.

Gone now are the days of Mario and A.J., of Bobby and Danny and of Little Al as a new influx of drivers have moved into the Indy Car spotlight. This new breed owes a very special debt of gratitude to the legendary drivers who came before them and really put this style of motor sports on the map.

Again timing plays such an important role in life and I feel extremely fortunate to have been able to get a behind the scenes look into the men and machines at the forefront of this form of racing's development. It was an exhilarating experience not to be forgotten.

THE WRITERS

VIC CARUCCI

WHEN I think back to my years at the EMPIRE Sports Network in Western New York I have very fond memories of our signature program, FAN-TV which aired Monday through Friday from 4:30 to 7:00pm. It was the most uniquely formatted show I had ever been involved with as we combined news of the day with "live" in-studio guests and call-in's from fans all over North America from Seattle to Nova Scotia. There was also a full half hour of straight local and national sports news, so it proved to be a challenging yet very exciting daily exercise.

One of my favorite parts of the program was the ability for in-depth discussion on a variety of topics with regularly scheduled guests for thirty minute segments on a weekly basis. And one of the best was my time sitting alongside longtime Buffalo News writer and columnist Vic Carucci who is as dialed into the National Football League as anyone in the media.

From the Buffalo News to being an active member of the Pro Football Writers Association of America and NFL.com, Vic has connections throughout the league and is always on top of the latest news in around the NFL.

We shared side by side seats for a couple of years at EMPIRE and through my producer Brenda Alesii, Vic would provide talking points that he thought were important for that week's appearance. Brenda would then pass along the topics to me for me to get familiar with and our editors would then put together footage of a particular player or team that could be inserted while Vic and I were discussing the subject.

At home you might have been thinking how do they have video of what these guys are talking about so quickly? Well, that's how. It came off week in and week out very seamlessly and with the added bonus of us taking calls from viewers on the topics at hand, there was a real sense of give and take between the two of us on camera and the individual on the phone with us. That's what I particularly liked about working with Vic. It felt more like a conversation between a pair of friends rather than an interview and only got better as time went along.

It was fun while it lasted until EMPIRE closed up shop in early 2005. I moved back to Pittsburgh and Vic spent some time with the Cleveland Browns website until returning to Buffalo in 2014. Cleveland's loss truly is Buffalo's gain with Vic Carucci back home where it all started professionally.

FRANK DEFORD

While Vic Carucci's work is well known around NFL circles, Frank Deford's comes on a completely national scale. From award winning books and articles for Sports Illustrated, to a regular morning program on National Public radio and television appearances as a longtime contributor for Real Sports with Bryant Gumbel on HBO, Frank is one of the most recognized talents at his craft.

Whether it is fiction or non-fiction, biography or novel, his ability to tell a story is simply masterful. He does with words what a great painter achieves with his brush or a concert pianist creates with his fingers.

BOB & FRANK DEFORD

Deford came to Buffalo for an appearance in late 2001 as part of a promotional tour for his latest book entitled, "The Best of Frank Deford, I'm Just Getting Started". We sat down in a corner of the restaurant high above the playing field for the minor league Buffalo Bisons. We had an enlightening conversation about his book as well as his thoughts on several national and local stories that were in the news at the time.

I told him of my reading just about every single piece he had done for Sports Illustrated as I have had a subscription off and on since August of 1970. In fact I have each of those weekly magazines neatly preserved in my basement from January of 1976 thru today. When he stopped smiling at hearing of such a collection, I told him of a few of my favorite articles he'd written and I believe he was impressed that I had such an interest in his work. I went on letting him know that from the time my dad started a subscription when I was only twelve, I was hooked on wanting to read and I believe that is something sorely lacking from the youth of today at that time.

From then on I was voracious in my quest for information and getting it from a book that I could tangibly hold in my hands and read at my own pace was a very personal thing. I know it is one of the traits that helped me in my own career and Deford readily agreed.

His book was full of inside information as part of biographies that he had written. Sports biographies make up the majority of my own personal library and I really connected with his. In fact, that is exactly what this book is made up of entirely. My recollections biographically of personalities I have interviewed.

And one of the best compliments I have ever received in my profession came just after our short time together. At that point Frank Deford beat me to the punch and reached out to shake my hand and softly said, "Thanks for a wonderful interview." It felt like an A+ on an exam and helped validate why I had chosen the profession that I was a part of

LARRY FELSER

Also like Vic Carucci, the former sports editor and columnist of the Buffalo News and nationally recognized NFL historian, the late Larry Felser, was teamed weekly with yours truly on FAN-TV. I can honestly say I loved Larry. He was one of the finest individuals in any walk of life that I have ever met and I will always value his friendship.

I was also proud to be a professional associate of this iconic figure. I did not realize that as a young man growing up about three and a half hours to the south of Buffalo, Larry was someone who I was regularly reading. No longer published, Street and Smith's annual football season preview magazine was a staple for me to get the inside scoop on every team as well as have complete records updated.

In my formative years and then into my career from the 1960's through the mid 2000's, I always wanted to talk to athletes and coaches and ask the questions that I wanted answers for. But armed with the latest stats was also a priority, especially before there was the internet and instant access to such things.

In today's world, if a football game is on television all you have to do is log into the team's official website for up to the minute stats and that is all this current generation knows. Years ago you had to wait for your weekly edition of the Sporting News for the previous week's numbers, or Street and Smith's for all the statistics for a complete season or entire history.

Larry was a Sporting News and Street and Smith's columnist I realized once we met and it is so much fun to go back to say 1977, and read what Larry had to say about the Bills and the rest of the AFC including my Pittsburgh Steelers. I also collect Super Bowl game programs and Larry's work is all over those publications.

And if you were not aware of it, he was one of only eight men to have covered each of the first thirty five Super Bowls before his retirement. That is amazing. Longevity and a passion for the sport made Larry one of the most trusted men on both sides of the fence. That is as a voice for the fans and confidant of the movers and shakers of professional football.

VIC CARUCCI, BOB & LARRY FELSER at Super Bowl 35 in Tampa, FL

He was there from the very beginning of the old American Football League that eventually merged with the NFL to start the 1970 season. In 2008, he sent me a copy of the last book he authored, "The Birth of the New NFL (How the NFL/AFL Merger Transformed Pro Football)".

Nobody in the media in Larry Felser's heyday had the connections he had inside the hallowed halls of pro football. He could dial up everybody from Vince Lombardi to Al Davis to Lamar Hunt on a moment's notice anytime he felt the need. Yet despite his ties all over the country, Larry was at heart a Buffalo guy. That was quite easy to see and he was very proud of that.

I personally enjoyed our many times on set together at EMPIRE and certainly at his induction into the Greater Buffalo Sports Hall of Fame in 2000. Of course being with he and Vic at the site of his final Super Bowl in Tampa in 2001 was memorable as well.

Larry Felser. Just by saying his name I am taken back to my days in Western New York. It was a most positive experience.

PETER KING

If Larry Felser was the ultimate insider into the world of pro football then, there is nobody that is more connected as a writer, television personality or online columnist in today's NFL than Peter King. Peter was a classmate of mine in the Class of 1979 at Ohio University as was Matt Lauer of the "Today Show" on NBC. Toss in another pair of fine nationally known writers in Jay Mariotti and Cleveland's Tony Grossi and I found myself in some excellent company that went on to highly successful journalistic careers.

PETER KING & BOB

The Super Bowl is the best time to renew acquaintances with media members nationwide because you are all herded like cattle from press conferences to Media Day to other league functions and at least during the day there is nowhere else to go. I would run into Jay and Tony and Peter fairly regularly, but Peter in particular because he would always make a tour of each NFL franchise during training camp. I would find out when he was coming to Detroit or Buffalo and arrange time for a quick hello to reminisce and then conduct an interview for his national perspective on those organizations.

In some form, King has been associated with covering the NFL for over three decades and his insights are must reading for millions of fans. He is the senior NFL editor at Sports Illustrated, an on set or in the field contributor to Sunday Night Football on NBC, and he offers his perspectives online at MMQB.com (Monday Morning Quarterback). He is usually spot on regarding a current situation or upcoming event and its projected outcome.

Peter King continues to be a leading conduit for inside NFL information. I just wish at times that I was still a colleague actively involved in the business so I could ask questions that have built up since my own departure from broadcasting in early 2005.

DICK SCHAAP

Much like Frank Deford, I also had tremendous respect and admiration for one of my journalistic heroes, Dick Schaap. Dick was always at the center of the action from his base in the biggest city in the world, New York City.

He was there for Willis Reed and the Knicks, Mickey Mantle and the Yankees and boxing's Muhammed Ali and Joe Frazier. Schaap was always on hand to lend his special gift of description and opinion.

I always enjoyed reading his columns or books and especially watching him as the inaugural host of ESPN's The Sports Reporters on Sunday mornings. He commanded the roundtable discussion with precision and for the most part I readily agreed with his opinions on whatever the sporting topic might be.

I was also fortunate enough to be able to host Dick on FAN-TV at EMPIRE just a few weeks ahead of Super Bowl 35 in Tampa which would prove to be the final Super Bowl I ever had the chance to cover or attend. He was in Western New York promoting his autobiography, "Flashing Before My Eyes: 50 Years of Headlines, Deadlines & Punchlines". It proved as usual to be a great read and it was compelling to hear him speak at length about the moments and athletes and coaches he had covered in a half century.

BOB & DICK SCHAAP

Honestly I cannot think of another sports media personality who has been on hand for more of the break though events of the Twentieth Century than Dick Schaap. For thirty minutes it was like going back in time as he offered insights on Ali, and a pair of Joes by the names of Montana and Namath who I was particularly interested in as both men are from my home area in Western Pennsylvania.

He ended up incredibly comfortable in the presence of presidents, movie stars and sports figures and was read nationally not only on the sports pages, but the news pages as well. A journalist in the truest sense of the word, it is especially nice to see his son Jeremy now carrying on a family tradition with his in depth reporting for ESPN.

If Roberto Clemente and Gale Sayers were my heroes on the field of play, then it was Dick Schaap journalistically. And I am so glad I was able to meet and interview him on "live" television before his untimely death. Eleven months later he was gone from complications following hip replacement surgery at the age of sixty-seven.

EPILOGUE

IT'S kind of funny how things seem to work out. Despite the fact I loathed math as a school subject, somehow some way, I actually became fascinated by numbers. The statistics I first saw on the back of my bubble gum cards as a kid eventually turned into an important and much needed part of my professional sports broadcast career.

That career feels like I just blinked and it was over. From the first paid day in 1984 at WILX-TV in Jackson, Michigan to my final time in front of the camera on the sidelines of a college football game in California, Pennsylvania in 2005, it feels like it went by so fast. My career lasted close to twenty-one years or approximately seven thousand five hundred days. Like I said, a blink of an eye.

Had it been physically possible, I most certainly would have continued my career to this very day. However, like so many of the athletes and coaches I interviewed over those years, I was forced to make some changes in my life's "game plan".

But if there is one message or lesson above all else that I want to get across to you as you close the page on this book, it is this. Dream big and under no circumstances let anyone tell you that you cannot do something. Whether it is literally trying to reach for the stars and become an astronaut or being the doctor that finally finds the cure for cancer, don't let anyone take away your dream.

In my case, the simple and obsessive desire to be actively involved in covering the games, the teams, the cities and mostly the individuals who play and coach sports in America was my dream. It can be done if you want it bad enough. Work, hard work with many missteps along the way will test your will time and again. A door will slam shut in your face one day, but the next you will be warmly greeted by new opportunities and challenges. I know firsthand. As a not so friendly reminder I have kept each and every rejection letter from news directors for positions I applied for. I could start a major fire with all that paper which kept me quite humble as I worked my way up the broadcasting ladder.

Each of us has a gift that was presented to us at birth. I am not a philosopher, but I like to believe in my heart that our whole purpose in this life is to recognize that gift and discover how to use it. And then reach down deep and make it a passion that will not be denied.

For me the bottom line always was and has been that at the end of the day, did I try my hardest to be the best at what I do? Did I find a constructive and positive way to overcome any obstacles potentially blocking my personal success? And while doing that was I a good person, a good employee, a good friend?

Teamwork and how you play your part on the team is very important to me. My individual abilities finding a match professionally to utilize them with the end result being a great interview or a compelling feature story became part of who I am. I took great pride in that each and every day I grabbed a microphone and a pen.

And oh yes, as dad would remind me relentlessly long before my career ever began, "There really is no excuse for not giving your all every day. It can be a scary place, the real world. But if you are a good person who cares about what you do and how you treat people along the way, you will go far. And have some fun while you are at it or what's the point?"

Dad, I got the point and can honestly say that I sure did have a lot of fun. Thank you.

ACKNOWLEDGEMENTS

I want to thank a few individuals who along the way at some point in time helped to drive me to not only start, but finish this project.

Bob Lemieux hired me right out of Ohio University in 1979. From the start Bob knew my goal was to get into broadcasting even though that was not the job I was offered upon graduation. But he opened doors in Kalamazoo that eventually led to my first full time sports position at WILX-TV in Lansing. He remains a dear friend to this day.

Former WZZM-TV News Director Jack Hogan's encouragement was a blessing in my formative years as an anchor and reporter. He played a big part in me gaining self-confidence. It wasn't always easy to hear, but the corrections I made were absolutely for the better.

Former EMPIRE Sports Network secretary Sandy Messore radiated light in the depression that immediately followed my heart attack in early 2012. Nobody pushed me harder to get what I had in my mind down on paper than Sandy. I was in a dark place and cannot thank Sandy enough for her love and support.

And finally my editorial adviser Joann Dobbie. My first draft was in need of "cleaning up" and Joann outlined my strengths and weaknesses as a writer, and did so in a most positive manner. The finished product you just read is the culmination of our work together.